(ME)VOLUTION

CHANGE BEGINS WITH ME

By Jon Duschinsky and Dr. Tony Myers

Tracy:

Pursue your dreams

Love life

Be true to you!

hugs

Tony@Myerslan.com

(me)volution – Change begins with me

IMPORTANT:

(me)volution is more than a book. A movement and a call to action, it confirms that each of us has both the ability and the tools to bring about the change we want to see in the world. The opinions expressed herein are solely those of the authors. To ensure the currency of the information presented, readers are strongly encouraged to solicit the assistance of appropriate professionals.

Further, any examples presented are intended only as illustrations. The authors, publishers and their agents assume no responsibility for errors or omissions or for damages arising from the use of published information or opinions.

ISBN# 978-1-895589-98-6   (me)volution – Change begins with me

Published by **Civil Sector Press**
Box 86, Station C, Toronto, Ontario, M6J 3M7 Canada

www.charityinfo.ca Telephone: 416-345-9403

Publisher: Leanne Hitchcock

Editor: Lisa MacDonald

Design: Ray Barrett

Production: Alan Tang

**For my children and grandchildren,
the next generation of philanthropists
and change-makers, that you may experience
the fullness of life, and love and transformation.**

Tony

**To Katerina, for bringing my guide
and soul-mate into this world.**

Jon

ACKNOWLEDGEMENTS

Our gratitude goes first to those who brought us the stories: Fraser Green, Ken Burnett, Tom Ahern, Kay Sprinkle Grace, Jana Ledvinova and Simone Joyaux. Thank you for sharing your stories of change and for the patience you showed as we grappled with the challenge of bringing them together.

We are equally grateful to Sam Singh, Ken Shipley, Karen Hlynsky, Noerine Kaleeba, Brother Kelly, Veronica, Mary-Kim and David Serra, for allowing your stories to be told and for teaching us so much about how change for good happens. Thank you for your humanity and for giving us such powerful examples to share with the world.

Our next acknowledgement goes to Jana Ledvinova from Prague, Czech Republic who, as well as being one of its contributors, generated so much enthusiasm when the idea for this book was first discussed that we just couldn't let it go. It is Jana we thank for lighting the fire of conversation that fuelled our enthusiasm to get the project off the ground.

Jim Hilborn of The Hilborn Group in Toronto for always being encouraging, always patient, always optimistic, and always determined that we should succeed. Thank you, Jim, for your humanity and your ethical leadership and for your commitment to supporting the work of the voluntary sector in Canada and beyond. To Leanne Hitchcock and Lisa MacDonald, The Hilborn Group, for your sense of humour, your hard work and dedication and for sticking with us until the end.

To Sonia Swiridjuk and to Renee Krysko who organized our lives and helped us drive the process in the early days and helped to get this project off the ground; your tenacity, kindness and friendship are cherished.

And finally to our families, friends and colleagues everywhere who have continually encouraged us in our work and in our pursuits. We are grateful for your support throughout this journey. You must know that if this book helps one person to change their world then it will be thanks to you.

CONTENTS

FOREWORD

by Jon Duschinsky and Dr. Tony Myers

This book is published in the context of an evolving new world order.

It is born into a world of uncertainty, where power is shifting away from heads of state, the institutions and powerful corporations and towards individuals like us.

It is such a different world from the one that welcomed in the new millennium, just over a decade ago. Governments, democracies and currencies are transforming. Rules are being unwritten and few in power seem able to take responsibility for re-writing them. Where will it end? How long will this carry on? No-one seems to know. And yet, despite the uncertainty, this profound shift in power and influence offers us unimaginable opportunities.

This new world order is based on a single, unifying global belief and a single unifying purpose: *philanthropy* – the love of humankind, and the inherent desire of the vast majority of us to foster change for good.

As human beings we are social animals, with a profound desire to communicate and live collectively. However, for most of history, the ability to influence the course of events and the world we live in has been restricted to elites and those elected to office.

No more.

Today's connected world is influenced less by politicians or "leaders" and more by individual human beings who, using the tools of our time (the tools made possible by technology and globalization) are taking the power that can bring about incredible change.

As we write this, Syria, Italy, Egypt, Greece and many others are all on the frontlines of this new world order. It is the people of these countries, the individual human beings, who are driving a new future for their societies, not the elected politicians, business leaders or technocrats. These great civilizations, many of which, over the centuries, have been synonymous with tyranny and absolute leadership, are now all being led *by their people* to reinvent themselves at the same time.

This is both the context in which this book is written and the ultimate reason for writing it - to help *us* understand *our* own power. It is a wake-up call for *us*, that we might realize that we have both the ability and the tools to begin a conversation for good that can ignite passions and set the world on fire.

But more than a wake-up call, it is a confidence-booster. For many of us secretly know our power. So this book shares the experiences of ordinary people who have changed the world, so that we can see the path and travel it ourselves.

This is the path, the journey of (me)volution.

(me)volution is a model of how ordinary people go from having a great, powerful idea about changing something, to building a movement that *actually* changes it.

It is about seeing and hearing how others have changed their world and mapping that experience so it can be shared.

And by sharing it, we hope that (me)volution will help you make *your* mark, build *your* legacy, and make *your* difference.

Because all change begins with me. Or in this case, it begins with you.

INTRODUCTION

Berlin, November 1989. Power fell and people rose.

It was a *moment*. It was a *movement*.

At some point in the life of every generation there are these *moments*, these *movements*.

We are taught that they define and influence our mindset, that they are part of our cultural and collective DNA and that they meld our history into the malleable truth we feed our children.

And they do.

But they are only a tiny fraction of the picture.

For in your world, *moments* such as these are occurring every day, initiated by ordinary people who have no inherent ambition to be part of history, but who exercise their humanity in the hope of leaving the world a slightly better place than they found it.

Every day, millions of people around the world do things that don't make the headlines and won't fill tomorrow's history books, and yet these same things may have profound influence on the way you live your life. Every day, ordinary people do extraordinary things that demonstrate courage, tenacity, unselfishness, vision, spontaneity and love.

Who are these people? Look around you. They are right there; on the subway, pushing a cart around the grocery story, walking along the sidewalk, picking up their children from your school. They are you. They are us. *We* are the people of whom we speak.

We – us – *people*. Empowered by technology and the unseen forces of globalization. Empowered by the diminishing role of government. Empowered by a collective consciousness that is calling out for change, and by a media that has force-fed us the cult of the individual until we have all bought into it. *We* are making change in unprecedented ways.

All around us, those who traditionally had the power, are floundering. Politicians, despite their desperate posturing, are impotent to master the global economic machine. Economists are trying to predict tomorrow's markets with theories that were written on parchment paper and charities are still making the same empty promises that we've been hearing for thirty years.

The institutions cannot be relied upon to create the solutions we need. The powerful no longer have the power. And we all know this.

So. What are you going to do about it?

This book is about addressing that question. It is about showing how you can take your power, about helping and challenging you to be part of the solution in ways that you have dreamed of but not yet realized. About giving you the tools you need to be the change you want to see in the world.

To do this, we should start by taking inspiration from iconic leaders of the last century. Some faces come easily to mind: Mandela, Gandhi, Martin Luther King, Ang San Suu Kyi, the Dalai Lama, Che Guevara, Desmond Tutu. Others are more difficult to conjure up, even though the names might be familiar: Vaclav Havel, Lech Walesa, Andrei Sakharov, Wei Jingsheng, Mohamed Bouazizi.

How are these people like you? Or more, how are you like them?

At first glance, you might not feel any particular commonality with an iconic leader. You might feel humbled by Mandela, rather than thinking of him as a peer. And as you go through the list – from armed revolutionaries to religious leaders, from trade unionists to physicists, you would be forgiven for seeing them in a different category. Away from mere mortals such as *us*.

But, what if these people had a commonality between them? Not in who they are but in what they have experienced?

What if there was something in their respective journeys that was the same, or similar, regardless of who they are and where they started?

What if there was, in some way, a common path that these leaders (consciously or unconsciously) followed?

And, *what if* we could all learn and gain insight from those experiences?

What if you, could be just like them, by being just like you?

(me)volution

We believe that there *is* a common journey that guides our iconic leaders and heroes. We believe that *they share a similar set of experiences and they have travelled a similar path*, much of it routed in philanthropy, the love of humankind.

We further believe that these experiences are not limited to the Gandhis and the Mandelas of this world. We believe that ordinary people are having them every day. And we believe that you can have them too.

These unrecognized heroes have much to teach all of us – and in recognizing their journey, we can find out where *we* are on *our* journey and find the inspiration to not rely on politicians and economists and third parties to create the world we want to leave to our children.

We are going to share the stories of eight people. Not eight iconic heroes who figure in history books, nor eight Nobel Prize nominees. These are stories of eight regular people who have each changed the world in a powerful way. Ordinary people who have made a big difference. Their stories illustrate, similar to those of a Mandela or a Luther King, a shared set of experiences that propelled them through their journey of philanthropic change – driven by a love of humankind and a desire to do something to make life better for someone or something.

This book is about them. And it is about what we can learn from them.

They are (me)volution. They've been through it. And collectively they'll show you the path.

But it is also about you, and your own personal journey.

As you explore the pages ahead and discover (me)volution for yourself, we think you will find both affirmation and encouragement. We hope that you will be able to recognize yourself through the experiences of others and that they will give you confidence to follow your dream, to articulate your vision for a better world and to go out there and make a difference.

We would love to think that we invented (me)volution. And in a way, we did. But really, it was gifted to us. We did no more than listen and learn from the stories of these eight people. And that in itself, may well be the biggest lesson we can all draw upon.

If you are already on the road to change, use this book to strive ahead, safe in the knowledge that others (and not just the people you read about in the history books) have been there before you. If you are just beginning, you now have a guide to take with you. May it bring you strength.

So what exactly is (me)volution?

Well, it begins with a *feeling*. A visceral experience. A sensation that wells up inside and forms itself into an idea that just takes over. Like a saucepan of milk boiling over on a stove. Seizing the heart, the mind, the nervous system. Becoming a conviction, a passion, a compulsion.

It is a feeling that "I need to do this" regardless of what "this" is.

We've all had these moments. You know what we are talking about. Maybe you saw a photo, a film, a documentary or a report. Maybe you heard or read something. It's often a reaction to the status quo or to an injustice. It may involve righting a wrong, correcting an injustice, protecting the environment, helping the hungry, healing the sick, saving a life or creating a vision for a better future for a single person, or a whole community. Or none of the above. But it's grabbed you. And you know you need to do something about it. And you know that you can be part of change.

And then it morphs.

It moves from a very personal feeling to something that you share. And when you do – when you share your outrage, your dream and your vision, you create the platform where you can bring people together. People who get it. People who resonate with the values you are sharing, who want to help you and be a part of whatever it is that you are doing.

And then, as a critical mass of people, energy and change builds, you empower others. You provide the tools for the message to spread, for the movement to build and for transformation to become possible.

This is the journey that cuts the pathway to every real change:

- A sensation that becomes an idea.

  - An idea that gets powerfully shared.

    - A movement that is empowered.

(me)volution has three parts to it:

I) The journey you take in yourself

The sensation takes form. It wells up inside you and begins to take shape – a desire to help, to do something, to take action, to change the status quo. You think about it, you form it, you move from initial visceral compulsion through a growing sense of conviction and confidence as whatever "it" is begins to become real.

II) The transition from you to others

You make it real – by doing something, taking that first small step towards changing the status quo. And by doing so, you make it real for others, who can join, who can embrace your vision and the values you are sharing and get involved too.

III) The journey others take with you

The idea grows into a mission or a cause that becomes bigger than you, that becomes about "us" rather than about "me." For no-one who has ever brought about change in the world has done it alone. They have done it by empowering and inspiring others.

(me)volution is about going from an individual passion to "do something", through the articulation and sharing of the idea, its values and vision with others, to the creation of a movement that transforms the life of a single individual or an entire world.

Whenever we set out to make change, when we draw on the love of humankind, we go through these stages. We believe they are universal.

(ME)VOLUTION MODEL

(me)volution is a journey and it is a model; a model of transformational change.

On the next page you will see the (me)volution model laid out in its entirety – all seven steps – from *Compulsion* through to *Empowerment*. As you move through this book and discover each step for yourself, refer back to this model. Use it as your guide.

So fold over the corner of the page so it's easy to come back to. Or, pop a yellow post-it note on it. Or, be very 21st century and take a photo of it. Print it out and stick it on the wall above the chair you're sitting on now. Use it in any way that takes your fancy - for it is *your* model, here to guide you on your journey

The journey you take in yourself

Tunisian fruit vendor Mohamed Bouazizi, 26, doused himself with gasoline and set the world on fire.

His protest was against mistreatment by local officials. His death in early January 2011 ultimately led to the fall of the government of President Ben Ali. This, in turn, stoked the confidence of people across the Arab world and set a domino effect in motion that has rewritten (and continues to transform) the political face of the Middle East.

A young Tunisian man experienced (me)volution. His compulsion to do something, to make his voice heard, and to make the ultimate sacrifice, gave the people of his region the compulsion, and in turn the confidence to rise up and reach for what they believed was justly theirs.

We have entered the era of (me)volution – an era in which opportunities and information flow in an unprecedented fashion, allowing the individual to instigate transformational change in a way that simply wasn't possible just a few years ago. We have been gifted the unique potential to change the world. Our voice matters. Dissatisfaction can be shared. An idea or vision can be shared and inspire others like never before.

In many ways (me)volution reflects democracy in its purest form. Instead of having to fight to fit into a centralized, vertical, hierarchical system, each and every one of us can be players. The days of professional lobbyists who lurk in dark corners of the corridors of power representing private interests rather than the public good may well be numbered.

Today, we can all be influencers, creating opportunities for a better society. We can channel that energy, that talent and all the time that people commit through philanthropy and volunteering, and amplify it without having to endure the pain of manoeuvring in a vertical system. We can set the agenda, confident that the policy-makers and the politicians will follow us.

(me)volution may well be the most important journey that any of us take. And when we engage in change, it is a journey that we *all* can take.

So let us begin it. The first step on this journey begins in a small village in India.

SAM SINGH'S
STORY

told by Tony Myers

The narrow dirt pathway inside the rural village could hardly be called a road, but it is! The open ditches along its sides channel a murky flow of human and animal waste out of town – some of it destined for streams and rivers, some for open fields where the rich liquid mix cultivates and supports vegetation. The vegetation supports the cattle. The cattle support the people by working their farms, pulling their two-wheeled carts, and carrying their provisions. This is cattle country. This is Uttar Pradesh, India.

In town, leading away from the narrow roads are a myriad of gateways – linked by stone and mud brick-walled fences that separate homes and tiny private yards from more public spaces. Some gateways are open, some are closed-off and barricaded by locked doors. Many lead into tiny enclaves where the modest and the poor live in crude shelters and opened-walled buildings they call home. The structures protect the people from the sun and rain and ensure air circulation when the temperature hits 50 degrees Celsius, as it often does.

Eighty percent of India's population lives in rural environments, under the rule of male-dominated households, in villages like Bichola where Virendra Singh was born in 1941. Virendra was luckier than most. As one of seven children of a lawyer, his upbringing enjoyed the privileges that come with being part of a well-to-do caste. He left his village at the tender age of ten, propelled by his parents to seek an education that ultimately led to an engineering degree from Punjab University, a master's from Lowell in the United States and a lifetime career at one of the world's largest corporations – DuPont, where he capped his career as President of the South Asia division.

Virendra Singh's story is not being shared here because he rose to the top from very humble beginnings, but because of what he is doing now. For after a successful career, and at the age of sixty, Virendra Singh is giving back. Not by doing anything as mundane as creating a foundation and sitting in leathered-up luxury while giving his, or someone else's money away. No, Virendra has returned to the rural villages of Uttar

Pradesh where he grew up. There, he has rolled up his sleeves to take on what he believes to be the biggest of all injustices and the greatest of all opportunities – education (or the lack of it) for young girls and women in rural India.

Opportunity knocks

"Call me Sam" Virendra Singh told me when I first met him outside the American Embassy in New Delhi. A slim, fit-looking sixty-something gentleman greeted me with a firm handshake and a mile-wide smile. His speech pattern was slow like a Louisiana farmer, yet as methodical and deliberate as an Oxford graduate.

When we went inside the U.S. Embassy for dinner, Sam welcomed me with the grace and charm of a diplomat. During his many years representing one of the world's giant corporations, Sam developed the poise and polish one might expect from a seasoned politician. But his road to the top was not without its challenges. He learned that he could find opportunity in the midst of challenge, an insight that would evolve throughout his life.

By his own admission, Sam was "a lousy student," but "good at sport," particularly field hockey. It was this sport that got Sam recruited to Aligarh Muslim University (AMU) where he played until AMU's arch field hockey rival Punjab University lured him away. There, Sam played field hockey until he completed an engineering degree in 1962. After graduation, he joined Delhi Cloth Mills (DCM) and quickly realized that if he was going to get anywhere, he needed more education.

Sam headed for Lowell, Massachusetts where he got his master's degree, completing a thesis focused on DuPont fibres. Not surprisingly, DuPont hired him and there he stayed until he retired as DuPont's President of South Asia in the year 2000.

Sports gave Sam an opportunity to get to university. University gave Sam an opportunity to get an engineering degree – the degree got him a job, the job spiked his ambition, his ambition brought him to America to study DuPont fibre and do a master's degree, and DuPont gave Sam a lifetime of work. Sam took advantage of each opportunity as it came along. He was observant and insightful. He listened to the opportunities the world offered him and he responded to them one at a time.

Opportunity taken

You see, if by any measure Sam Singh is judged to be successful, it will be in large part because throughout his life he has seen and acted on opportunity. He is an opportunist and has been since the earliest days of his life. What is unique about Sam is that he can actually see opportunities. It is not to say that he doesn't see the obstacles as well. It is just that the opportunities seem to stand out. It is Sam Singh's ability to see opportunities and his ability to muster the courage to act on those opportunities that eventually brought him to philanthropy and philanthropic work.

In Sam's mind the economic development and social well-being in rural India, and in particular, Uttar Pradesh, is key to India's future. And he sees the education of girls as the single most important factor in securing that future.

The moment of truth

While still working with DuPont, Sam had occasion to meet with a client in New York. He was welcomed by the receptionist, offered a coffee and provided with a newspaper while he waited for his client meeting.

"If I'm not mistaken, it was *The New York Times*," Sam recalls. There, on the front of the newspaper was a picture that would forever imprint itself in Sam's memory. It was an image of an old woman rummaging for food in a pile of garbage. Near her, a tiny girl, maybe eight years-old, rummaged through the same pile. Also framed in the photo was a sacred cow, picking away at the rubbish. It conveyed, in shocking form, the reality of life for many women in India.

Sam looked at that picture. He more than looked at it. He stared at it – couldn't take his eyes off of it. His mind was racing.

"I started to think about the business meeting and the client I was going to be meeting with. What is she going to think about the picture and about me as a man from India?" Sam wondered. Shortly after seeing that picture for the first time, Sam walked into his meeting with a white Anglo-Saxon American business woman for what, he told me, would be the longest meeting of his life.

"For the next hour and a half," Sam confessed, "every time she finished a sentence I thought the next question would mirror the thoughts that were running through my mind. 'What is Sam doing in this country and why does he not go back to India and why does he not do something about the picture?'"

"When I saw this picture, it made me feel awful. It was the circumstances surrounding the picture that caused me to think about it so much." Sam was embarrassed. As a proud member of the DuPont executive team, he wanted to impress his client. As an Indian man, he wanted to impress the American woman. "But," he admits, "I was already being 'sold' by the picture on the front page of the newspaper." The world, he surmised, already had an impression of him. His only thought in the meeting was how do I get out of here?

As it turned out, the woman in the meeting never asked Sam the question that he was so afraid of. She never mentioned the photo or questioned Sam about it. Nevertheless, the image lingered in Sam's thoughts. He wondered about the photo, and the young girl whose plight was destined to be the same as that of the old woman.

He thought about the work of Mother Theresa in the slums of Calcutta. He questioned himself. He questioned India. He wondered why India could not produce its "own Mother" and why it had to import Mother Theresa from the "outside?" Indians are wealthy. Why couldn't he and the people of India do something so that young girls and old women didn't have to pick through garbage to survive?

Sam Singh resolved to do everything in his power to change the plight of girls and women in his homeland. He decided that as soon as his youngest daughter got a job and became independent, he would leave DuPont and return to India.

The front page of The New York Times had changed Sam Singh's life forever. The compulsion to act was so powerful that he felt he simply "must" do something.

It took ten years for that "something" to take shape.

In December, 1999 Sam gave notice to his boss. His last working day with DuPont was in March 2000. Within four months, Sam's first school for girls opened its doors. Forty-five students showed up for the first day of classes.

Pardada Pardadi Educational Society (PPES)

"Pardada Pardadi" literally means great-grandfather and great-grandmother. In the village of Anupshahr there is a wall in the central square showing a family tree that traces Sam's heritage back ten generations and identifies his great-grandparents by name and shows the family tree. Sam's name is located close to the bottom.

It is in the village of Anupshahr where one of Sam's three schools exists. It is where his dream to change India was to unfold. It is there where Pardada Pardadi Educational Society was to be born.

In India there are only 933 women per 1000 males. It is a country, Pardada Pardadi Educational Society claims "where girls face discrimination from the womb to the tomb." Their right to life, health, education, livelihoods and freedom of movement are at the mercy of patriarchal society.

Uttar Pradesh, where Sam's schools for girls were to be located, is one of the least developed states in the country. It houses 16% of the total population of India – 80% living in rural areas. It claims the highest growth rate in the country, yet there are only 898 females per thousand males as compared to the national average of 933. The literacy rate in the state is 57%—only 43% for females. About half the districts in Uttar Pradesh show less than 20% literacy rate and in some pockets there are villages with zero literacy.

The situation with regard to scheduled castes and other lower castes is even worse. The percentage of school-aged children (6-10 years old) attending school is only 37% and for children aged 11-13 years old, only 53%. Girls comprise only 29% of the population of 6-10 year olds, and 39% of those aged 11-13 years.

Poverty; the inaccessibility or non-availability of schools; the low value accorded to education by the community; the poor quality of teaching and learning; gender disparities; class and caste discriminations; and a lack of employment opportunities are just some of the significant challenges facing the region of India that Sam calls home.

Anupshahr is a part of the district of Bulandshahr and is comprised of a largely rural population. In Anupshahr there are more than forty thousand families whose monthly income is less than 400 rupees per month (equivalent to $8.40 US). These families are the target population for the Pardada Pardadi Educational Society (PPES) programs. PPES works with girls from 46 villages. It is here that Sam would get his first taste of success in his new venture and his first experience with failure.

Facing adversity

To realize his dream, Sam started with a school for girls in Anupshahr. To encourage girls to attend the school, Sam personally visited almost every family in the region, talking to the mothers and convincing them to send their "girl child" to his school. The mothers were reluctant. Families couldn't afford to lose the free labour, and dispense with the contribution the girls made to the family workload and income.

So in return, Sam promised the mothers that he would provide each girl ten rupees a day for every day they attended the school. Initially the money was given to the girls at the end of each semester – an approach which turned out to be disastrous.

In addition to being paid a stipend for attending classes, the girls were given uniforms, three meals a day, books and school supplies and, for those who lived further away, a bicycle to get them to and from school.

In 2001, enrolment at Sam's school was 45 girls. After only one semester, almost 60% left and many sold their uniforms and bicycles. The approach, as generous as it was to the girls and their families, failed. Sam had to do something different.

Instead of paying out the stipend at the end of each semester, Sam decided to pay out the money to the girls after graduation. As a result, the girls would receive approximately 50,000 Indian rupees (US$ 1,000) when and if they graduated. Now there was a compelling reason to stay and finish their schooling.

The change of student incentive resulted in a more stable enrolment. Now, the school has upwards of 1,200 students, (phenomenal growth in a short period of time) and the dropout rate has been reduced to a trickle. Initially, many might have thought the experiment a failure and been tempted to quit. Sam faced the adversity, saw an opportunity to change his approach and made the changes necessary for success.

What started as a moment of truth in a New York office building in 1989 has turned into a life-long conviction to bring change to rural India by providing girls with an education, teaching them independence and increasing the likelihood that they will be able to economically support themselves. If Sam is successful, there will never again be a picture like the one Sam saw on the front page of *The New York Times* depicting an old woman, a young girl and a sacred cow foraging through garbage for life and sustenance. Sam's unwavering commitment to educating Indian girls has the potential to create a movement that will change the fabric of Indian society forever. It can only happen, admits Sam, one girl child at a time.

Success has many faces

"Let me tell you about Asha," says Sam.

Asha came to school when she was seven years old. Every day Asha was the first one to school and the last one to leave. Sam found out later she begged her dad to let her come to school. She told her father that she would continue to do all the work at home and in the fields and that her dad wouldn't have to spend a penny on her education.

Asha continued her education and as a mature teenager, got an opportunity to visit the United States. It was during her time in the States that she saw, among other things, people getting married on a Saturday completely contrary to common practice in India where most people only get married on a Sunday. The visit to the U.S. and the educational opportunities that Asha was given, gave her the confidence to make her own decisions.

After returning from her visit to the U.S. and graduating from Pardada Pardadi School, Asha decided independently to marry a man of her choice. She decided independently to marry at a time and place of her choosing. And, had she wanted to, she would have married on a Saturday, just like they did in the U.S. but as things turned out, she got married on a Sunday – but, only because it was the day her friends could attend the ceremony.

For Sam, Asha's story is a clear example of success – an Indian woman, making her own choice of mate and getting married at a time and place of her choosing. More than anything else, Sam's dream for Indian women is to ensure they can make independent decisions and take care of themselves socially, culturally and economically, with full access to personal and financial well-being without fear of repression from fathers, family or husbands.

"Our basic objective is that every girl child will be socially and economically independent," says Sam. "The Indian girl child has been locked in rules for hundreds of years where she is required to be married at a certain time to a man determined by others. She is only allowed to go where her parents think it is safe for her to go, where her brothers think it is safe to go. Asha stood up in front of the village and in front of her family and said 'I will not live this way.'"

"I've always said that there is no magic. If you give human beings an opportunity to stand on their own feet they will do it. Even the girl who is collecting grass for cattle and collecting the wood for cooking, she can be anything."

Sam also tells a more sombre story of Rehana – a 13 year-old girl who was destined to be married to a 40 year-old bachelor. Because her mother was mentally challenged, Rehana was raised by her elderly grandmother. Her grandmother's greatest fear was that if she died, Rehana would have no-one to care for her and would end up in a brothel. Being married to an older man was the lesser of two evils.

"You don't like what I am doing?" exclaimed Rehana's grandmother to Sam. "You can take her as your daughter or your wife or in any other relationship." So, Sam took Rehana under his wing and supported her as his daughter. Success comes in various forms, with various degrees of commitment and various degrees of personal sacrifice.

From great solutions come even greater challenges

With over a thousand girls coming to school every day, one would think that Sam has made it – that he has achieved his goal and realized his dream by founding an institution that will, in time, bring change to the entire district of Bulandshahr. But, as often happens, solving one problem can create new ones. This is exactly what happened in Anupshahr.

Girls are now graduating as young women. They have gained a sense of self. They are, in many cases, the first women in their family to graduate. The challenge is that there are now independent-thinking young women who don't want to be dating the boys from the region, because the boys are either uneducated, or not educated to the same level as the girls. By creating opportunity for girls, Sam and the Pardada Pardadi Educational Society have upset the social balance.

For most, this would be a problem. But for Sam the opportunist, he only sees problems and challenges as opportunities in waiting. It is a simple matter. If boys need better education, you open a school for them too.

"I have not changed my focus on education for girls," says Sam. "What I am doing is maintaining balance in the community so that the girls can continue their education and so that we maintain harmony in the social fabric of rural India."

And where do Sam Singh and Pardada Pardadi Educational Society go from here? "We need a hospital," says Sam. "We need a hospital."

A hospital is only the next step. It is not Sam's ultimate goal. He sees yet another opportunity, bigger than anything yet realized. Before he dies, says Sam, "I want to say I put a model in place that transformed rural India."

So, in the beginning Sam opened his girls' school. And now more than a thousand girls are getting a chance to dream, to hope and to project themselves into another reality.

One thing has led to another. Because the educated girls don't want to date boys who aren't, Sam is searching for more solutions. And because educated girls who want to be doctors also need a place to work and make their own change happen, more searching and planning and solutions evolve.

In fact, what is striking about Sam is how his journey, starting with a moment of compulsion to do something, has grown into a powerful, life-altering vision – to initiate a movement for transforming rural India, one girl-child at a time, village by village, region by region.

COMPULSION — "I MUST"

Sam's *compulsion* and first step into the (me)volution journey started with a photo that created a visceral feeling of disgust and shame. When Sam gets that initial feeling, he has no idea what he's actually going to do. But slowly it comes together. Slowly an idea forms and takes shape and ten years after his first moment of compulsion, Sam was back in the village where he grew up, laying out plans for his first school.

You never quite know when *compulsion* is going to hit.

Instead of a retirement spent at the country club playing golf, Sam decided to go out and change the world. By all measures, Sam is an ordinary man, who had a moment of compulsion that has resulted in thousands of lives being changed.

The feeling of *compulsion* experienced by Sam is not uncommon. In fact, we believe that all of us will, at some point in our lives, experience something akin to what Sam felt on that day in New York City. It can take different forms. For some, it may emerge out of a feeling of revulsion. For others, it begins as a fascination, or a calling. For others still, it manifests as an absolute driving need. Whether it's a reaction to something heard, something read, something seen or maybe something just imagined, it hits you between the eyes. And you can't ignore it.

The first step of (me)volution is an intensely personal experience. It can be a visceral, identity-defining, rising-from-the-gut-and-wrapping-itself-around-your-neck kind of experience. It is *not* a shared or communal experience (at least not yet). It is more like a hyper-virus, penetrating your soul from an outside stimulus and settling there, multiplying at an exponential rate so as to quickly become all encompassing. It is a "strong, irresistible impulse."[1] And it is the root beginning of all fundamental change.

Every non-profit organization in the world was created by a man or a woman who experienced a moment of *compulsion*. This is not a revelation, it is a simple truth. Every non-profit has a founder whose moment of *compulsion* led them to want to do something, to change something. And from that desire the organization was created.

The word c*ompulsion* has a powerful incarnation to it with both strength and immediacy. Yet, let's be clear. Moments of *compulsion* can be earth-shattering, smacking you in the middle of the forehead like a truth you have ignored for years. But they can also creep up on you, a faint tickle to the back of your neck, causing a slow awakening.

However it happens, what is important is that it *does* happen, and that at the end of the experience of *compulsion*, we have a new awareness that leads us to embark on a journey of change.

But (for there *is* a but) if we have all experienced *compulsion*, why have only some of us done anything about it?

Why is it that some of us fall off the precipice of procrastination and end up ignoring our moment of *compulsion*, while some of us embrace it and change the world?

What is it that makes Sam Singh decide to change the course of his life, while so many of us have a great idea and then go back to our day-jobs?

Obviously, there are a number of things at play here. Obviously, *compulsion,* the first step of (me)volution, is but the spark to a brighter fire.

---

1 http://www.dictionary.com

KEN SHIPLEY'S

STORY

told by Fraser Green

"Nothing worthwhile is too much trouble."
- Edna Shipley

Ken Shipley came into this world on October 5, 1932 in a remote location called Shellmouth, Manitoba – on the Canadian prairies. His beginnings were far from auspicious.

Manitoba is a harsh place in many ways. Temperatures in the winter can reach –50 degrees Celsius · and the summer's heat is equally brutal. The land floods in spring and bakes in summer. Snows are deep and the wind always seems to howl.

Ken's mother, Edna had to take the train to a neighbouring town to deliver her firstborn. On the return journey to Shellmouth, the engineer failed to stop at the station and Edna and her new baby were dropped off several miles down the track to walk back. An early winter storm had dumped three feet of snow on the ground. So began Ken's life.

Ken's parents lived in a small cabin outside the village. They hauled water. They split wood. They struggled for simple physical survival. Ken's mother would keep his baby bottle under her pillow in the winter – only to wake in the middle of the night and find the milk in it frozen solid as her baby cried with hunger. Edna would put Ken on the kitchen floor to play while she made supper, but first she would bundle him up in his "outside winter clothes."

Ken's early years coincided with the Great Depression and during that time, the Canadian prairies were the hardest-hit region of the country. In that area, severe drought had crippled agriculture (the primary economic engine of the region). Coupled with the financial crisis triggered on Wall Street in New York, times were beyond hard.

Ken's parents did everything they could to sustain themselves and their two children. They farmed the land they rented around their cabin. They were butchers. On weekends they worked as auctioneers. Ken's father Rollie was also the bailiff for the area, which meant he had to execute foreclosures on farmers who could not repay their loans and mortgages to the banks.

Rollie and Edna were poor. They were uneducated yet they gave freely of themselves to build a community. Edna was active in church affairs, was a regular Sunday school teacher and organized sock-knitting projects for Canadian soldiers during WW2. Rollie served on the local school board and despite his rather difficult responsibilities as bailiff, earned a reputation for fairness and listening before acting. Ken was not blind to these behaviours.

The harshness of that time in history – both in terms of physical environment and economic calamity – bred a unique culture of community on the Canadian prairies. People learned quickly that cooperation and community were essential to survival. Out of this culture, a strong farmers' cooperative movement was founded that survives to this day.

Ken's parents instilled in him a set of beliefs and values that have served as the moral compass of his life:

- Everyone – regardless of gender, race or economic circumstance – is worthy of dignity and respect.

- Being fair in all your dealings with people is the bedrock of trusting relationships.

- Love your neighbour as you love yourself.

- Giving to others isn't an occasional luxury – but rather, it's a moral imperative.

Acting in accordance with these beliefs has created the true meaning to Ken's life.

In their classic fundraising book *The Seven Faces of Philanthropy*, authors Russ Alan Prince and Karen Maru articulate the seven fundamental motivations for giving.

Of these seven, Ken clearly embodies two. He is an altruist in that his giving – whether of time, talent or treasure – simply feels good. He is also a communitarian in that to him, it simply makes common sense that we can accomplish more together than we can individually.

The ticket beyond

Despite his family's meagre resources, Ken grew up in a family rich in reading. Ken's mother had taught school before having her children – and she read constantly to Ken and his sister when they were little.

His maternal grandfather was a voracious reader, despite only four years of formal education. Ken's grandfather would scour used bookstores during his infrequent visits to Winnipeg and return home with leather-bound copies of Grimm's fairy tales, Charles Dickens and Emily Bronte. Ken still has many of those volumes on a shelf in his home.

When Ken was quite young, he was encouraged by the family doctor to limit his reading due to advancing near-sightedness. He ignored the advice and used to hide in closets and the barn so that he could escape to faraway places and times with the characters in his imagination. This, he believes, sparked his interest in the world outside northern Manitoba.

Formulating a world view

Ken is the first to admit that he was a late-bloomer in terms of his social and political beliefs – and in the activism they led to.

He obtained a university degree in agriculture, married Carol Bowyer and moved to Saskatoon, Saskatchewan to take up a career as a mortgage officer with a major trust company. Ken and Carol began a family and settled into the normalcy of family life.

In his early thirties, three events occurred that triggered Ken's transformation from husband and father to citizen of the world.

In 1961, the Government of Saskatchewan enacted the Medical Care Insurance Bill which would guarantee universal access to healthcare to all Saskatchewan residents. This legislation was repudiated by the province's doctors, who felt that it would strip them of their freedom to practice and would ensnare them in a communist-like regime. The province's doctors went on strike in 1962 and the province was deeply divided on the issue. Ken very strongly sided with the Government's position and his communitarian instincts began to take on political overtones.

A few years later, Ken and Carol were asked to take on the leadership of a United Church youth group known as Hi-C. On Sunday nights, forty or more teenagers would meet in the church social hall under Ken and Carol's direction. Ken and Carol developed a strong rapport with these young people and tried hard to respond to their needs by truly listening to their comments and requests. The experience was incredibly rewarding.

Ken and Carol would consult their teens on programming – and soon found out that the kids were particularly interested in sex. So, they brought in guest speakers and engaged the teen membership in discussions about sexuality. This was in 1964. The minister, church elders and many of the parents were outraged that their children were "allowed to be exposed" to such discussion. Ken and Carol staked their turf on the side of the teenagers. Their advocacy and activism had begun.

At the same time, Ken was asked to join the Saskatoon chapter of Canadian Crossroads International – a Non-Governmental Organization (NGO) that sent Canadian volunteers overseas to work on international development projects. Membership on the local board involved both fundraising and volunteer recruitment and selection.

Ken fell in love with this role. As he participated in interviewing candidates to go overseas, he found himself hungering to go and do this work himself.

It was also at about this time that Ken came to a fundamental realization about his life. His career enabled him to do the volunteer work that he truly loved. Work fed his family. Volunteering fed his heart and soul and gave meaning to his life.

Ken's career continued to evolve. He earned a Master's Degree in Education from the University of Saskatchewan and began working for its extension department – bringing agricultural innovation and improvements to the poorer farmers in the region. He also began working with aboriginal Canadians, which ultimately led to Carol and him adopting an aboriginal daughter after having three children of their own.

Ken also became active in the Lerner Centre movement – dedicated to bringing international development education to ordinary Canadians. His interest in, and passion for, international development work continued to grow.

You want to do what??

1977 marked a turning point in Ken's life.

At the age of 45, with four teenage kids at home, Ken approached Carol with an off-the-wall idea. What if they packed up their lives and went to work for a few years in Africa? At first, Carol thought Ken was off his rocker – but soon she became infected with the idea.

They jointly applied for a position with CUSO (founded as Canadian University Students Overseas) to manage its field operations in Botswana – a landlocked country on the northern border of South Africa. After some reluctance because of the children, CUSO accepted Ken and Carol to share the position (the first time in Canada this had been done). They packed suitcases and trunks, sold their house and headed east on the greatest adventure of their lives.

They settled in Gaborone, and took on the task of managing forty CUSO volunteers who were engaged in teaching, providing primary healthcare, business consulting, agricultural development and water engineering.

According to Carol, Ken put his own stamp on his work immediately. He showed patience uncharacteristic of white development workers at the time. He always took the time to listen to local people and really consider what they had to say. The Batswana[2] people took to him and accepted him right away. He earned a reputation for quiet effectiveness and perseverance to see jobs through to successful completion. His quiet style and innate respect for the views of others (which he'd learned from his parents) served him well.

Carol describes Ken as "ecstatic" during those years. She says he was simply in love with his work and the people he was working for, and with. "He took to the place and the people like a fish takes to water," she says with a huge grin on her face.

Today, more than 30 years later, Ken and Carol can vividly describe the place and its people in sensory detail: the sound of clunking cowbells everywhere; the incredible body odour of villagers who hitched rides down the dusty roads between villages in the CUSO Land Cruiser; the taste of grilled chicken and maize in someone's back yard on a Sunday afternoon; the instant, cool relief of stepping into the shade of a tree after broiling in the afternoon sun; and, the sight of an acacia tree in the desert against the backdrop of the gigantic orange setting sun (they have a large photo of such a scene on their living room wall).

During his time in Botswana, Ken was an instrument of change. He played a pivotal role in the early days of the movement to bring Batswana people into staff and leadership positions in development projects and added volume to their voices in decision-making.

---

2 Batswana is the name given to the people of Botswana

Ken and Carol were also sympathetic to the African National Congress (ANC) movement in South Africa. During the late 1970s and early 1980s, the liberation struggle pervaded all aspects of life in the countries of South Africa, Botswana, Zimbabwe, Mozambique and Namibia. We're all familiar with Nelson Mandela's 29-year imprisonment on Robben Island – and his non-recriminatory approach upon achieving power. Ken was amazed and impressed that people who had been so subjugated could be focused on solutions and not vengeance. This sat very well with his practical prairie upbringing.

One day, a knock came on Ken and Carol's door. A friend had come to ask if they'd be willing to risk harbouring two ANC activists who were being pursued by both South African and Botswana police. Without hesitation they agreed, first giving the couple safe refuge and then helping them escape to Zambia and Canada, where they live today.

Ken and Carol feel they accomplished much during their three years in Botswana. But, they're quick to refute the idea that the experience was that of "giving." They both feel strongly that they were the receivers – of experience, knowledge, wisdom and great love. In their minds, they took away more than they came with. I admire that in them.

"I've got four teenagers. I certainly don't need a maid!"

"Do not wait for leaders; do it alone, person to person." - **Mother Theresa**

When the Shipleys arrived in Botswana, they inherited the house of their CUSO predecessor, complete with a twenty-three year old domestic worker named Regina. To Ken, having domestic help was an ostentatious show of wealth and privilege – it just rubbed him the wrong way. So he informed Regina that he didn't require her services.

She protested vociferously that she wanted the work, that it was a good job and that she had no other place to live but the little shed in the back yard that served as the maid's quarters. Ken and Carol offered to let her stay in the shed until she could find new employment and offered to help her look for work.

It wasn't long before Regina found work with another North American family. But soon she was back to Ken and Carol, telling them that her new situation was quite abusive and that she was very unhappy. During the conversation Regina also told them that her dream had always been to finish her high school education.

On the spot, Ken made Regina an offer. He and Carol would pay her maid's salary and give her back the maid's quarters but instead of cleaning floors and cooking meals, she was to go back and complete high school. Regina beamed at the offer, and accepted it immediately.

Regina went back to school and graduated. She then got a job she loved as a guide at a museum – at triple the salary she'd been earning before. Through that experience, a friendship was formed that exists to this day.

Regina eventually married and had four children. She wrote the Shipleys back in Canada regularly and even phoned once in awhile. When her husband was killed in a car accident, Regina went through a financial crisis. Once again the Shipleys went into action – calling and emailing friends to ask for their help. The response was immediate – and Regina's life was put back in order.

Today, Regina's four girls are grown, educated and all have well-paying jobs that they like. The girls look after their mom, but Regina still writes or calls Ken and Carol every now and then to say hello and to remind them how much their help has meant to her over the years.

Ken doesn't see anything special in this story. He simply crossed paths with a fellow human in need, so he helped out to the degree that he could. That's just his way. After all, his mother always used to say that "anything worthwhile isn't too much trouble."

Regina, on the other hand, would tell a much different story. A story of how her life was transformed because of this wonderful couple from Canada who took the time and trouble to care about her and invest in her future.

You can't go back

"Only a life lived for others is worth living." - **Albert Einstein**

Ken and Carol Shipley (and their four kids) were changed forever by their years in Botswana. The world had become their neighbourhood, humanity; their family. This remarkable couple developed the capacity to take the world and its people into their embrace and to hold that embrace until this day.

Ken joined CUSO's Canadian staff upon his return, as Deputy Manager of Overseas Operations, responsible for CUSO projects and programs in 45 countries around the world.

In the late 1980s, he took on the mandate to build CUSO's fundraising capacity – and grew the program to a revenue level approaching $4 million by 1992. During this time, Ken became one of the first Canadian fundraisers to get active in the then-emerging field of planned giving (in fact, he was my first planned giving mentor).

His volunteer involvement accelerated as well. Ken was active with the Saskatchewan Council for International Cooperation – and later served on the Board of Directors of the national body of the same name. In the 1990s, Ken was Volunteer President of the Canadian Seniors for Social Responsibility and was a board member for Broadcasting for International Understanding. In 2001 and 2002, Ken co-facilitated an innovative training program for South American NGO fundraisers in Sao Paolo, Brazil.

He is still active as a board member with Peace Brigades International Canada and is the Chair of the Board of the Peacefund Canada Foundation. In 2008, (at the age of seventy-five!) Ken became a founding member of Atzin Canada – an NGO that supports indigenous peoples in the state of Guerro, Mexico.

Ken has, of course, also been a very active donor to charities and causes all his life. He just doesn't like to talk about it much. Suffice to say that over the years he and Carol have given tens of thousands of dollars away simply because people needed their help. Ken probably isn't ranked as a major donor by anyone. His name probably doesn't appear on any tribute walls and no one has ever held a gala black tie event in his honour. Ken is simply way too good at flying under the radar for that kind of attention. But he has given generously and consistently - decade after decade after decade.

Meaning makes the wheels go round

Ancient Egyptians believed that the dead were asked two questions at the gates of heaven:

"Did you bring joy?" and *"Did you find joy?"*

It's pretty clear that Ken Shipley has done both – big time. Ken radiates the simple joys of being alive and being able to get involved. Activism and involvement are everything to him still, and anyone who knows him can see that he has a pure and simple gift for giving joy to others.

Ken's children are grown and they have all inherited the spirit of giving and involvement – each in his or her own way – from their mom and dad. Ken and Carol are the proud grandparents of seven grandchildren – who are, in turn, beginning to show signs that they "get philanthropy." This is a great source of happiness for Ken who believes that "they're going in the right direction."

Ken was asked, "if you reached back into your life and removed all your volunteer and philanthropic experiences, what would be missing from your life?" He responded simply. "It's not a question of what I'd be missing. What would I have left? What kind of father would I have been? What kind of grandfather? Who would my children and grandchildren have become without all that?"

Is that not the essence of philanthropy and meaning?

Ken Shipley has dedicated his life to change and the betterment of the human condition. He has worked tirelessly for decades in this single-minded pursuit. He has enjoyed his victories quietly and endured countless setbacks without grumble or complaint. Ken has a Buddha-like understanding that true satisfaction comes not from the destination but the journey.

And yet, he would tell you that he did not give endlessly. In his view, he was rewarded for his efforts and contributions every step of the way.

Ken Shipley is truly a noble and humble human being. He is an inspiration and role model.

Ken Shipley is a man who has changed the world, who has touched lives and who feels that it was all entirely natural.

He is someone we would all like to know. An unsung hero who would blush at the thought that he was being called such a thing.

COMMITMENT – "I WILL"

If (me)volution is about being able to effect change without necessarily having to give up your present "ordinary" life and transform your current existence, you might be wondering why you have just read a story about a man who not only gave up his day job, but also moved his entire family to Botswana, to follow his (me)volution!

Bear with us…

Ken was brought up with conviction by his parents. As Fraser tells us, he was instilled with "dignity and respect," with the importance of "being fair to all," of "loving thy neighbour" and with the knowledge that "giving to others isn't an occasional luxury – but rather a moral imperative."

But the world is not short on people who believe things but don't act on them. Just because we are instilled with beliefs in our tender years, or educated in a certain way, doesn't mean that we are going to do anything about them.

The key here is that Ken acted on his convictions, just as Sam Singh did. But, he acted somewhat differently.

Sam felt a very personal *compulsion* and vowed to change something, but it took him a further ten years to arrive at the place in his life where he moved the vow into action. As he sat in that meeting room in New York City, he didn't know what he was going to do, or how he was going to do it, or even when "it" would happen. But he knew he had to act. It was a compelling need that was stronger than any other he'd experienced to that point.

Ken's story doesn't focus on the onset of his *compulsion*. Rather, it demonstrates to us the importance of a growing *commitment*.

Once we've been struck by *compulsion*, we have to begin to frame whatever "it" is, into something we can move forward. And that is where the second step in (me)volution comes in. As illustrated by Ken – great change does not happen immediately. Instead, it only germinates in the instant of *compulsion*. The seed is planted but it is a phase of *commitment* – fostering the feeling that "I will" do something that causes movement to happen. And, as Ken's story shows us, this can take quite a while to grow and flour-ish. And, it can also lead us to some remarkable and unexpected places.

"I will" is the first expression of a positive, constructed action. It is the first step away from the precipice of procrastination towards the altar of action.

You are no longer in the adrenaline rush of *compulsion*, but in a more composed, collected state where determination has set in and where *commitment* (even a slightly mad one, such as going to Africa with four kids) forms.

Sam Singh taught us *compulsion*. Now Ken Shipley has illustrated the second step - *commitment*.

Commitment follows *compulsion*. An individual experiences a reactive moment of *compulsion* which leads, over time, to the *commitment* to follow through on the idea instead of dumping it (like a piece of trash) into the place in our consciousness where we store our "if only I could…" thoughts. These are the ideas, when revisited with age, that can lead to a sense of regret that certain challenges were never even attempted.

"I must" – even if I don't know what it is that I actually have to do, nor how I have to do it

+ time

leads to "I will" – where I grow into a deeper understanding of what it is that I want to do

As you go through this second step of (me)volution, it is up to you to decide the scope of what you want to do. It is up to you whether you want to quit it all and disappear with your family to a village in Africa, or if you want to do something more modest (but no less valuable) that will fit within the constructs of your existing life. This is not a decision that other people can make for you, nor is it a decision that you should delegate to anyone else. It is up to you to decide what your (me)volution looks like. It is you who will *commit* to something once it feels like it is achievable.

We are not all Mandelas or Gandhis, nor should we pretend to be, or aspire to be. But just because you are not prepared to risk your children's education by getting sent to jail for a cause you feel compelled to do something about, does not mean you can't make a difference to your cause. Maybe even a critical difference.

You choose. It is your (me)volution. It is your commitment. Make it work for you.

But even after *commitment*, we still have a gaping hole. Even if you develop a deeper understanding of what it is that you want to do, the question remains - can I actually do it? This question is both fundamental and critical. Without the belief that "I can," both *compulsion* and *commitment* will fail to lead to *confidence*, the next step in the (me)volution journey.

NOERINE KALEEBA'S

STORY

told by Ken Burnett

Noerine Kaleeba is a beacon of hope in the battle against HIV/AIDS. As well as being the founding force of The AIDS Support Organization (TASO) in Uganda, the first Chair of ActionAid International, a board member of AMREF and Marie Stopes, a world-respected expert on HIV/AIDS, an adviser to the UN and head of the FONK and GURU programs for disadvantaged children, she is mother and sole-provider for at least 40 children, only four of whom she gave birth to herself.

Each day, she dedicates herself to giving them the best start in life that she can.

Enough is always a relative term and in Noerine's world there is always much, much more that needs doing. So, no feet up by the fireside for this African granny.

Noerine Kaleeba had to battle ignorance, taboo and stigma before she could start the first support group for AIDS sufferers in Uganda. Yet with little more than self-belief and the goodwill of friends she created a movement which began to turn the tide of AIDS as it swept through Africa. But instead of resting, Noerine then took on another social taboo - dedicating herself to creating opportunities for Uganda's disadvantaged youth. And that's not all.

Self-confidence is every would-be world-changer's secret ally. It's the crucial internal in-gredient in the make-up of anyone who would achieve great things. Most of us struggle to deploy at least a veneer of self-belief and succeed or fail to varying extents. Noerine Kaleeba found herself confronted by horrendous, overwhelming obstacles yet, thanks to her extraordinary self-confidence, went on to truly change the world.

The master communicator

It still flabbergasts friends and family when they see the influential circles in which Noerine routinely works her magic. It comes as no surprise to find her in the presence of world leaders, presidents and prime ministers. U.S. President George W. Bush met

Noerine twice, and she became a good friend of Britain's Prime Minister Tony Blair, who once personally cooked her dinner. Noerine shares international platforms with UN heads, government ministers, officers of states, stars of stage and screen and top figures from NGOs and civil society. They all seek not just her guidance, advice and opinions but also her approval and her company. Yet Noerine keeps them all in their proper place, for the company she enjoys most of all is that of her family and friends. There are plenty of them and they keep her very busy indeed.

Noerine is driven by a simple logic fuelled by openness, humility and an unshakeable belief that it's quite simply her duty to get her story across to anyone and everyone who will listen. So she takes her message, in the same way with the same power and passion, to people of the highest and lowest stature. Her mission is simple – that we must stop this nightmare, AIDS.

That's why you're likely to see Noerine take the microphone on the world's stage, to hear her speak out fearlessly on what world leaders must do to protect their people. But you're equally likely to find her squatting on the floor of a mud hut in Zimbabwe, Ghana or wherever, exchanging jokes and stories with survivors in "positive lives" groups, encouraging and inspiring the voiceless and the marginalized to stand up for their rights and for their children.

Noerine Kaleeba is a modest human being. She has become a great international figure in the fight against AIDS and a great inspiration to poor women everywhere, particularly African women. But she did not seek this greatness, rather it was thrust upon her from the moment she refused to quietly accept the inevitability of her husband's death, refused to accept the taboos that surrounded and stifled discussion of the issues raised by his death, and rejected the passive denial of reality that society expected of her and sought to impose at every turn.

So Noerine noisily embarked on a role that cast her as spokeswoman for previously voiceless AIDS families, the forgotten bereaved who up until then could only mourn in isolation and bleak despair. Noerine was impelled by events outside her control to find strength and power within herself, then to use that, triumphantly, to influence other people to take a stand. With Noerine as their leader, the previously powerless families have achieved extraordinary things. But, though she may have inspired them, Noerine would not wish to claim sole credit for these achievements.

Noerine isn't just a great leader and a wise adviser; she is also a terrific dancer and enthusiastic celebrator of life. Actress Emma Thompson, who since travelling with Noerine in Africa has become one of her closest friends, summarizes why, of all her attributes, "self-belief" best describes her singular contribution to philanthropy.

"Noerine has an inexhaustible belief in and talent for being alive," observes Emma. "The first thing she did upon arriving in Kampala with me was to visit her niece Harriet, who is HIV-positive. Harriet told Noerine she was dying. 'Until you die,' growled Noerine, 'you are living. I will remind you that you live with AIDS.'"

This then is not a story of a vision, nor of a dream. Noerine is a very practical, down to earth person. She rolls up her sleeves and does what needs to be done. Her story is real, more shaped by a nightmare than any dream – the nightmare of AIDS that threatened to destroy a generation.

To respond to this threat she had to overcome her humble origins, cultural inhibitions and natural shyness and speak out about her most intimate experiences in a way that would be listened to, where it mattered. The inner-strength and self-belief that underpinned this defiant stance took her from an obscure Kampala suburb to a prominent international role in the fight against AIDS.

But Noerine had little choice in this. She had to do it.

One child in a million

Noerine was one child in at least a million, just in her part of Southern Uganda; a fertile, bountiful, beautiful land that overflows with sunshine, greenery and eager, vibrant people.

Within a day's walk of where Noerine was born and grew up there were countless others just like her, all equally poor, all equally deserving and needy. All, like Noerine, jostling for space and attention and resources and opportunities and the chance of making something, anything, from the tough cards that life had dealt them, seemingly from the bottom of the pack.

What made young Noerine stand out so, from this crowd?

Self-confidence, perhaps. And a talent for speaking out for what's right.

For Noerine Kaleeba, third oldest girl in a family of 11 siblings and 16 half brothers and sisters, growing up amid the poverty of rural Uganda meant dreaming of a better life - but how unattainable that dream must have seemed.

By Ugandan standards, Noerine's father was not a poor man. However, he had four wives, and Noerine was a child of wife number four. There were always so many brothers, sisters and cousins around that it was hard for Noerine to get any attention at all.

There isn't so much as a brick left standing from the single storey shack where Noerine was born, more than fifty years ago. All that remains is the scorch mark of foundations, a stony shadow on the ground a few feet long and a few more wide. Barely enough room to swing a cat, far less to raise a family from the small parcel of bright red earth that's around.

Noerine doesn't remember much of the hardship of her upbringing, but she does remember developing an important survival technique from an early age. Young children waiting in line to be fed would often drift off to sleep as they waited. But if you fell asleep you would miss your turn and no one would wake you because it was assumed that, if you were asleep, you didn't really need food. So Noerine learned that if she was feeling tired she should move to that place on the floor, in the corner of her family's hut, where they would need to place the food. That way, when the food came, the adults had to wake her, to get her to move out of the way.

Noerine was smart, resourceful and industrious, so she grew up strong and fit. She wasn't the most beautiful of her sisters so her father, who with his four wives had many calls on her time and responsibilities, decided that if she was to survive and thrive she couldn't depend on finding a husband: she needed a professional education and a job.

Noerine settled on physiotherapy and became rather good at it. Before long she was specializing in orthopaedics, physiotherapy and community rehabilitation at Makerere University and was going on to complete her studies in England. Not long after returning to Uganda she was made head of the School of Physiotherapy at Mulago teaching hospital, Uganda's finest, in Kampala. The career ahead of her seemed strenuous and challenging enough, but then Christopher, Noerine's husband, fell ill.

First encounter with AIDS

Some months before, Noerine had accidentally come across AIDS. Though its impact at the time was limited, its effect on her later was profound. Noerine explains in her book, *We Miss You All*.[3]

> "I had gone to one of the medical wards in Mulago to locate a patient for a practical demonstration for physiotherapy students on the techniques of transferring a paraplegic from a bed to a wheelchair. I found a young man who couldn't have been more than thirty years old. I introduced myself and explained what I required. He was very receptive and gave permission

3 Kaleeba, Noerine and Sunanda Ray. (1991). *We Miss You All*. SAfAIDS.

for my students to learn from him for that afternoon. His medical notes indicated that he had paraplegia due to Immuno-suppression Syndrome, but I didn't know what that was. I went to the ward sister to get permission to teach the students on her ward that afternoon. She came closer to me and said, 'I wouldn't touch him if I were you. He has AIDS. We don't touch him, we only show his mother what to do.'"

"I did not use him for the demonstration. Neither did I go back to him and explain that I would not be coming. I cancelled the class and arranged for another patient from the orthopaedic ward."

"I did not think about him again, until the diagnosis of AIDS came through my front door. Today there isn't a day that passes when I don't wonder what happened to him. With whom did he carry the burden? What friends did his mother have, with whom to share her emotions? How much did he know about AIDS? What support did he have? I will never know."

This wasn't an easy time for anyone in Uganda and the Kaleeba family was no exception. But Noerine merely nods in passing to these troubled times.

AIDS came into Noerine's life – right into her house – on the 6th of June 1986, the day that she received the fateful fax from the British Council in Kampala telling her just how sick Christopher really was. Until then, she had no idea what might be wrong with him. "There was no reason whatsoever," Noerine explains, "to associate my husband with a white homosexual disease from San Francisco, which was all that we in Uganda knew about AIDS then."

Wife, mother, caregiver, counsellor

Noerine and Christopher had met and fallen in love as students in the early 1970s. Both spent time away from home, studying and gaining qualifications to secure good jobs upon their return.

It was on one of these extended study tours that Christopher took ill. Though he had been complaining of poor health and lack of appetite for some time, Noerine was not told how ill he was until he was very ill indeed. Then she was flown to England to be at his side. Christopher was clearly dying, but his first words to Noerine were, "What took you so long?"

It became clear that Christopher had contracted AIDS from a blood transfusion following a road accident. When the call for blood had gone out, his younger brother Godfrey had offered some of his. Godfrey died in 1984, an early, undiagnosed victim of AIDS, one of the first in a long line of tragedies for the Kaleeba family.

Speaking out and inspiring support

"I didn't know the magnitude of the stigma associated with AIDS, so I told my neighbours and friends at work. I told my in-laws and my parents. I told anyone who came to sympathize with me."

Noerine realized that fear of this unknown killer had spread through her country like wildfire, that fear combined with two traditional Ugandan taboos – sex and death – had come together to make AIDS the disease that no one dared to speak about. So Noerine brought it all out in the open, from the start.

In 1987, The Aids Support Organization (TASO) received its first funding from the international NGO ActionAid, who ran it as if it was a department of the charity. Action Aid had listened to Noerine and assessed her as sincere, determined and "with a sort of substance that's rather hard to describe," says Colin Williams, ActionAid's director in Uganda at the time. He gave Noerine and TASO, £5,000 to start and carte blanche to do with it what she thought best.

"Nothing ever fazed Noerine," Colin says. "She was able to present herself as totally up to the task on the international stage and completely humble and close to the local community at the same time. Hence the tears in the audience every time she spoke, which was every chance she got. Noerine's real skill was to spot opportunities, then mobilize and inspire a local support group to get cracking. She was extremely good at listening intently to, and seeming to agree with, my rational advice, and then would do something completely different. She was able to trust me to back her, personally, and never to seek to push ActionAid or myself into the limelight. Equally I was able to trust her to be wholly focused on building TASO without ever knowing exactly where it was going."

TASO delivers, when and where there's most need

A bright white four-wheel drive Mitsubishi truck with big blue letters emblazoned across it bumps and bounces along the rutted dirt track that takes visitors to the village of Malombe, Northern Uganda. Every week TASO workers deliver a cocktail of anti-retroviral drugs to 24 year-old Thomas, who lives in Malombe and has been a patient of TASO for six years. On the way they perform a similar, equally life-saving service for many others. Like Thomas, they all depend upon this delivery.

Twenty years ago, someone with Thomas' disease would already be dead. Even ten years ago, the future for Thomas would have looked bleak and short. Now, well...who knows? The chances for surviving and leading an enjoyable, useful life are high. For Thomas and for hundreds of thousands like him, the drugs that TASO dispenses have changed everything. TASO's nearly one thousand vehicles are delivering this miracle now, today, tomorrow and every day, to hundreds of thousands of AIDS survivors across Uganda.

Even now it's hard to recall how bleak things were for people with AIDS and their families in Uganda, before TASO. Those caught up in it seemed to be witnessing the slowly building massacre of Africa's youth. Infection was a death sentence. Stigma, superstition, fear and social exclusion were inevitable companions. Even discussion was taboo. For those lucky people who stayed healthy the sensible course was to entirely reject their sickly loved one. The only other option would lead to their own rejection, plus the dark despair of impotently watching a slow and painful death while sitting bedside. Many took that easy option rather than be tarnished by the nightmare of AIDS.

Today, TASO is a household name. It is one of the leading examples in AIDS care and support, having treated more than 200,000 AIDS patients across Uganda.

The presence of self-belief

When ActionAid needed suitably qualified Africans to join its new international board, Noerine accepted eagerly. I visited India with her just after this. In Uttar Pradesh we met the Musahars, the rat-eaters, landless labourers of the lowest caste who seemed to have nothing at all. They were living in rickety shacks on land owned by someone else, reduced to eating roots and rodents for survival. The scale of poverty shocked Noerine.

As we traipsed round the endless parade of villages surrounded always by a sea of eager Indian faces, there was almost total indifference to me, the solitary white face in the crowd. But there was endless, vocal curiosity about this huge African person with the closely cropped hair of a man, but the voluptuous, reubenesque proportions of a matron of a certain age. "Who, or what, is it?" they all exclaimed in shrieks of delight. Struggling in her wake to keep up, I have seldom felt more superfluous.

My favourite outing with Noerine was to the wedding of a friend of hers in Kampala. Ugandan weddings tend to be elaborate, sumptuous affairs with huge white marquees, massive crowds all done up in their Sunday best, bands playing, men in shiny black suits with big flowers and large numbers of colourfully-attired Ugandan women each displaying their best "gomesi," the bright, shiny dress with large pointy shoulders crossed by a radiant, satin sash. The bride was lovely and the groom suitably dashing, but we were the centre of attention. Noerine had to make a speech, but she insisted in clutching me closely to her throughout. "That way," she chuckled, "they will all think you are my mzungu toy boy. And it will EAT THEM UP!"

And it was true. Throughout the ceremonies until our furtive early departure, every eye was upon me. I have seldom felt so famous, so envied.

The mother ship

If you are lucky enough to meet Noerine Kaleeba you'll be impressed by a large imposing figure who, upon meeting you, quickly breaks into smiles and laughter. So your first impression, not inaccurate, will be of a jolly, laughing, overwhelmingly positive African "mama."

Family ties are strong in Africa so it's not unusual for orphans from AIDS and other illnesses to be cared for by a relative. In addition to her own, Noerine has at least forty other children that she is bringing up, the majority orphaned by AIDS. The children's names read like a roll call; Betty, Tonny, Sandra, Josephine, Tadeus, Nicolus, Henry, Prossy, John, Ivan, Lydia, Stella, and on the list goes. And on.

Noerine isn't just giving voluntarily of her time, talents and wisdom to TASO and other favoured causes. She is truly a major donor for these children. To pay for their upkeep and education, she simply gives everything she has.

Noerine and her supporters are well aware that it would take a really big miracle to solve Africa's great problems. That seems unlikely. More likely, the future solution will come from lots and lots of little miracles, like the ones Noerine is raising now. All that's needed is a mechanism that nurtures and develops in young Ugandans the combination of leadership skills and personal qualities that have made Noerine Kaleeba what she is – a beacon of hope in Africa.

CONFIDENCE – "I CAN"

Noerine is a bit of an exception in this book because she is a world-changer who has been recognized for what she does by world leaders. She gets invited to the prestige tables and to important international meetings. But there is something about Noerine that makes you feel like you know her. Maybe it is the way she never loses her focus on the really important stuff. Or, maybe it is her good humour.

When Emma Thompson talks about Noerine visiting her niece, dying from AIDS, it is clear from her "growl," that this African mama expects others to fight with the same determination that she has fought. She doesn't expect them to give up, just as she has never allowed herself to give up.

Noerine has self-belief. Oodles of it.

Perhaps it's in her genes; born in the struggle to beat-out twenty-five other hungry mouths for food. Likely, it was sharpened through the loss of her husband. Whatever the reason, Noerine has the "crucial internal ingredient in anyone who would achieve great things." The story doesn't tell us where it came from. But it does tell us that it is there.

It is confidence. It is the feeling that "I can" that represents the third step in (me)volution.

"I can" or confidence, is the profound understanding that you know you can do it (again, whatever "it" is and whatever scope you have given it).

- Step one: Feeling a *compulsion* to act. The feeling that "I must." This is where the motivation comes from.

- Step two: Developing the *commitment* to act, expressed as "I will." This is where you pledge to yourself to do something in the future.

- Step three: Feeling the *confidence* - "I can." You realize your ability, (at every level) within yourself to actually make a commitment to action.

Without *compulsion*, *commitment* and *confidence*, there can be no action.

In the same way that you've probably had a moment of *compulsion*, you may also live with a *commitment* to do something – "some day." But for so many, that day never really comes. Why? Because we don't really believe that we are up to the job. Because we don't believe that we can. Because it would be biting off more than we could chew and it feels too big and too scary. Maybe we haven't really scoped it properly and found the "it" we feel comfortable in achieving. Maybe because anything smaller than transformational just feels like a waste of time – we feel we have to go big or go home. Maybe we simply don't trust ourselves enough, or we are scared of how it will change our relationships with others, or unbalance that fragile thing we call a comfort zone.

Yet the reality is that we can take heart from Sam Singh, Ken Shipley and Noerine Kabeela, for they have shown us that when we have the *commitment* and *confidence* to take forward a *compulsion*, the world becomes a better place for it.

Sam Singh did follow through on his moment of *compulsion* when he left DuPont after his daughter got a job. Ken Shipley also followed through on his *commitment* to take his wife and four teenage children to Botswana. Noerine did struggle through the loss of her husband, mustered the *confidence* to act and became one of the most influential and powerful voices in the fight against AIDS.

These three people (note: people, not iconic heroes) mirror ourselves and our lives - our dreams and our frustrations. They have shown us that, yes, it is possible. Together, they have provided the model. They are our guides. May they inspire you to find the confidence to turn "someday" into "today."

THE TRANSITION FROM YOU TO OTHERS

The first three steps of (me)volution involve a profoundly personal experience. They are all about you – about the self and an internal journey to action. However, thoughts alone have never changed the world. Not without being expressed. Not without being shared, and not without being acted upon.

The fourth step marks a turning point. It is the point of transition. It is the point where the personal, internal journey moves to being something external that others can begin to relate to. It is the transition from you to others. While others cannot see our thoughts, they can see our actions. They can relate to them and they can want to emulate them.

Action is a word that is endowed with so much meaning. It is the cry and credo of the film director, of the military commander, of the corporate leader. We seem to live to achieve it, to define it and let it define us. Almost as if all of our being was pointed towards it.

So why is it that we collectively spend so much time debating whether we should take action? In fact, why do we spend more time talking about doing things than in actually doing them? Why are we so practiced in finding reasons to *not* take actions and in creating elaborate strategies to "put things off?"

All roads lead back to the precipice of procrastination, don't they?

Across the globe people sit in meetings categorizing actions and then associating things like "risk profiles" with them in an effort to ensure that the right actions are taken at the right time in the right way.

OK, agreed, if you are running a nuclear power station, it is best to ensure that you are doing the right thing at the right time. But really, for the rest of us – we have to stop this nonsense.

Collectively, we spend more time planning for action, strategizing about action and writing pages and pages about how the action might look (should it actually take place) than we actually spend doing things.

"Doing" doesn't have to be complicated. It doesn't have to be big and scary. It can be simple - tiny, even. It could even be a micro-action. You don't have to have a perfect plan to take the first step. For it is only a step. In the next story, Karen Hlynsky shows you that actually doing something, however small it may seem, not only makes a difference, but also starts something really powerful and exciting.

KAREN HLYNSKY'S
STORY

told by Tom Ahern

Part 1: E-mail from Sierra Leone

My trip to Sierra Leone started on an interesting note. The flight to London was pleasant enough: no waiting line at Logan, and time enough to sit down for a meal. My movie choice on board was Benjamin Button—a long film that took half the night. That and the meals and drinks made the flight go by quickly. At Heathrow, misdirection from airport clerks put me on a bus hunting for the BMI desk which I finally found at my third terminal.

The flight from London to Freetown was more eventful than the first. My assigned window seat in the last row was already occupied when I got there. While waiting in the galley for a new seat assignment, Loretta, the stewardess gave me glass after glass of water and talked about preventing malaria in Sierra Leone. I soon saw that the middle seat in the row I'd first been assigned was taken by an African criminal whose hands were crossed in front of him and cuffed to the men on both sides.

After drinking more water than I needed, I was seated in the row to the front and left of the trio. I could clearly hear that the criminal was not a happy guy. He began to moan more and more loudly until the passengers in the rear third of the plane stood up, stretching around to see what was going on. His wardens tried to calm him, urging him to consider that they were trying to help him and that he'd already been in prison for five years. And did he want to calm down or to return to prison? Obviously what he wanted was off the plane. He struck one of his captors—the one in my assigned seat—with the only weapon he had, his mouth. He bit into his head.

With all my rubbernecking it was hard to tell what happened next. It seems that there were actually three wardens in the last row—the third sat on the other side of the aisle. Airplane security hustled to the rear from the front of the plane. A couple of very, very large men from airport security showed up to block my view. Next thing I knew, the fellow in "my" seat raised his poorly bandaged head, looking like a sheik in a dirty disheveled turban.

It was off the plane and back to prison for the unhappy guy with sharp teeth. Loretta, the stewardess with water and a fear of malaria, told the passengers to lean towards the windows as security disembarked with their prisoner. We lost no time scrunching away from the aisles, but then relaxed when airplane security offered another plan and opened the back door to exit through the galley. We waited for the takeaway shuttle to arrive and watched as the wardens took the prisoner out backwards down the steps and away. An hour and a half had passed. The water Loretta had given me was working its way through my system.

Because a passenger had left the plane, protocol demanded that all of the baggage on board be accounted for. One by one the overhead cabinets were opened, and one by one the carry-ons were matched to passengers. Meanwhile, Loretta's water had reached its final destination. We were still on the ground and would remain there for yet another 15 minutes while a medical helicopter flew in the skies outside Heathrow on its way to a serious roadway accident. Takeoff couldn't happen fast enough. Once in the air I stared the seatbelt sign into darkness and hurried to the toilet for sweet relief.

My companion on the flight was a lovely Sierra Leonean who was returning home to visit after a ten year absence. He'd left during the war, made his way to Kenya, Guinea, and finally to Australia where he'd settled with his wife and 16 year-old daughter. He was nervous about returning to a new Sierra Leone that he wouldn't recognize, sure to find gaps in his past circle of friends and family. He spoke of the different life he had in Australia and how his daughter was growing up to be so modern, confidently growing into a young woman with schools that supported her choices—a far cry from the way he'd been raised. He'd left school having memorized his way through his classes to graduate without the skills or confidence to be self-sufficient in the world.

We talked about my project that would help transform the schools into places where teachers would facilitate learning—not teach with the cane; where classrooms would be learner-centered, not teacher-centered, and where students would learn life skills, citizenship skills, and entrepreneurial skills to help them grow to be fully-functioning adults. His obvious pleasure at hearing this made me realize how important this work is. It can be tedious and overwhelming, but so many people now working in Sierra Leone have taken on transformative projects that in a few years—or maybe the next generation—will shift the way people see themselves and their potential as human beings. So I'm ready to get on with it again.

Travel from Lungi Airport was by helicopter—a noisy, seven-minute trip over the bay to the heliport, where I was met by one of the International Rescue Committee (IRC) drivers I knew last year. He took me to my new home at the Pentagon, a five-level building full of IRC ex-patriots, where no one had a key to let me in. While waiting for Audrey to show up, I walked to a nearby kiosk to spend Le2500 of my remaining Le3000 on the most essential thing—bottled water.

I've arrived to a very different home. In 2008, I lived in a spotless, air-conditioned third-floor flat with interesting views from every direction. The balconies from the living room and bedroom overlooked the little Cole Farm neighborhood with all its friendly children.

My current three-bedroom ground floor flat has been reserved for transient workers - people who come into the country for a week at a time, or for those who have meetings in the capital before going back home to the provinces. Being here for ten weeks makes me a little less transient, so in my honour they got a new gas canister for the stove and a promise to fix the refrigerator. In the meantime, the kitchen has a large deep freeze that freezes what's on the bottom and chills what's in the trays on top. The air-conditioning only circulates unconditioned air and I was disappointed to find that the entertainment center (a monitor and an old VCR) won't play the DVD's I bought at a discount in Heathrow. At least I can play them on my new computer.

Even all this could be overlooked, but on opening the double metal doors to the living room the place smelled badly of mildew and the bare light bulbs hanging from the ceiling made the flat look dingy. In fact it is a dingy place. As I walked around touching my surroundings my hands turned black from soot. Soot on curtains, window screens, and mosquito nets, grime on walls, kitchen counters, and tile floors. The place is covered, not merely with the red earth dust that blows in the dry season, but with years' worth of uncontrolled automobile exhaust. I had a choice: I could become one of the ex-patriots who go to restaurants every night, returning home only to bathe and sleep, or I could tackle the grime and try to make this place a home.

By the time Radha and Barrie returned home from their night out I'd made my decision. I was the woman to clean this place up and make it into a proper B&B for transient ex-pats. And when Barrie said I probably couldn't get it cleaner than it was, I was determined to prove her wrong. Still wired from the long flight, I found cleanser and an old sponge and began with the kitchen counters and cupboard doors. I worked for a couple of hours until the lights went off at midnight and saw the counters come to life and a few inches of one of the brown cupboard doors turn the color of cream. Yes, it could be done.

On Saturday I visited my Guinean tailor friend who was very happy to see me. His joy and the smiling eyes of his wife and niece gave me the lift I needed to get to the market for more water and a few provisions. Then it was off to the Lebanese "pie" café for a sit-down lunch of freshly made pita bread and a zattar-veggie roll-up; down to the town of Lumley for a piece of Dutch wax print fabric to hang on the walls; and to the large Freetown Supermarket for proper scrub brushes, sponges, detergent, and food for breakfast and snacks.

Back home I scrubbed the kitchen cupboards and counters, took down the badly stained curtains, washed the kitchen screens and scrubbed half the kitchen floor. Radha and Barrie were surprised at the transformation. But now, my hands are sore, and I've had my fill. When I meet the "house-keeper," I will give her daily deep-cleaning chores to do - teach her if I must, so that this place reflects light again. There is potential here: three comfortable sofas are in good shape, a large dining room table, comfortable padded wicker chairs, and a balcony with a small table and chairs that faces the water a half-mile away.

Now, if I can deal with the noise. At ground level I'm close to the generator that runs from 7 to 12 pm plus 12 to 4 pm on weekends. What will be harder is the Christian preacher man on Wilkenson Road. He preaches the worst kind of fear-of-God Christianity with the worst kind of screaming voice using the worst kind of bad loudspeaker. Just as I found my earplugs (that his voice still penetrated) the whole congregation broke out in song. I may have to escape on Sunday mornings like Barrie just did. Sunday morning in the Pentagon will not be pleasant. When did he start? Nine o'clock? When did he end? 12:30? Yikes!

I managed to nap with earplugs before going out to buy mobile phone minutes, visit with the market lady who reprimanded me for not telling her I was leaving five months ago, and walked five minutes down the road to my former home at Cole Farm to see my old neighbours. The fellow who sells Nigerian DVDs came out to greet me. Hawa's face lit up, and her children jumped around me. I distributed three of the soap bubble wands that Dennis and Jamie found at a flea market. They were a big hit. Within minutes the soap was gone, blown to the wind, or spilt on the ground; but for a few precious moments the children squealed with joy.

Hawa's new concrete house is as I left it five months ago. She is still waiting for a door and windows. I hope to find out her story when I go back on Monday after work to meet with Andrew, the former security guard at the now vacant Cole Farm building. (It seems that the roof of the building is leaking.) He will know where the other guards—the ones I used to chat with at night—have gone. And I'll find out how well he's been doing with his computer classes—the ones I paid for.

Still searching for unsweetened boxed juices imported from South Africa, I went to yet another supermarket and saw a friendly American-looking person. (What is it that makes us recognize one another, differentiating from Europeans?) We both hesitated, then quickly introduced ourselves. She happens to be from Meadville, Pennsylvania. I got her phone number and promised to be in touch as she hurried off for a gathering.

Back at the Pentagon it has gotten quiet at last. I mention to Ibrahim, the security guard here, how much I enjoy the quiet. I say the noisy ministering in the morning is far too loud. He tells me that the whole neighbourhood is disturbed by him. He says his own type of Christianity is quiet, between him and God. I suggest that I go tell the minister and ask him to turn down his loudspeaker so we can get close to God in our own way on Sunday mornings. He says he will go. I suggest we go together. With a bit of advocacy and elbow grease in lots of directions perhaps I can create a comfortable life at the Pentagon after all.

Two days in, the lights will go off in eleven minutes and I have forgotten to buy candles. And so it begins again.

– Karen

Sierra Leone, 2009

In a hot, humid, scarred and hungry land, Karen walked toward the workers' canteen to eat lunch. Right there – wanting a meal and having food available – put her in a small minority. Sierra Leone is among the poorest places on earth.

A decade of civil war has driven a third of the population into refugee camps and disrupted everything. The country has become notorious for the blood diamond trade and squads of child soldiers: abducted teens and pre-teens, fed unlimited cocaine, speed, marijuana, and booze by their masters, armed with the legendary AK-47 assault rifle and sent out to terrorize.

The Kalashnikov, as it happens, is perfect for the young ones. It is light and reliable. It shoots ten shots a second; try to tap your finger that fast. The intention? Dominant firepower at close range. Anyone, no matter how small, traumatized, or wasted, can lock a clip into an AK-47 and unleash a shocking amount of savagery.

That was then. Since 2002 there's been a peace. Some may even consider it progress.

As of December 18, 2008, the standard Human Development Index – measuring such things as educational attainment, life expectancy, and GDP per capita – ranked Sierra Leone last among 179 countries. (i.e., the least developing.) Corruption wilts all that it surveys. Most people have no work. Elders are rare. The average lifespan today in Sierra Leone is about 41 years, about half what someone born in Japan enjoys.

Karen works as an education consultant. She is an eager, small, white, college-educated American in her late 50s. Like a lot of American NGO workers, she is ex-Peace Corps. Aid agencies flock to Sierra Leone. They want to raise the smashed school system up off its knees. Her hope comes with a shrug. The CIA says illiteracy among the country's females currently runs around 75%. Males do better, of course. But not all that much. It will take time.

In the U.S. she lives in a battered urban neighborhood, much declined from its snooty roots. There's a soup kitchen a few doors away; in the current bad economy, it's attracting record crowds. She's tried to sell the house for a year, but the real estate market is dead.

In Sierra Leone, Karen resides and works on NGO row. She's part of a small elite: well-housed, well-fed, well-paid, safe enough. Working there has had a surprising, pleasant side effect, too: Karen no longer takes her homeland for granted. She's a reborn America booster. Thanks to her long, on-the-ground exposure to Sierra Leone's limitations, she now deeply appreciates the industrialized world's functioning infrastructure, where things more or less work as designed, more or less on demand.

The guard at the canteen looked conspicuously ill.

Karen got up close. His eyes were doing funny things. "You're sick," she advised him. "Go see a doctor." He replied that he'd be fine, thank you. So she argued. But he refused to leave his post. A post abandoned means automatic dismissal in a country where most are unemployed. There were always a hundred people ready to replace you.

So okay. Understood. Karen walked off to grab lunch in the canteen.

When she came back, the guard looked far worse. He was going down fast. She saw it in his eyes. He had collapsed against a tree trunk in the shade. She lifted his chin. His head was light as a sheet of paper.

He looked at her through a glaze, determined until his last breath to fight for his paycheck. He had a family.

"You need help," Karen said.

He barely nodded.

She proposed, "After your shift then."

"I can't afford the doctor," the guard whispered. He wasn't asking. He was dismissing her; that was that. There was no real hope. She was a stranger. In a land with nothing free or easy, he expected nothing.

Karen pressed the back of her hand against his forehead. It was hot as an electric iron.

"How much?" she asked.

He mentioned a small figure.

Karen rustled through her pockets. She found a few bills and coins, the equivalent of five dollars U.S. She stuck them in his jacket. "You go to a doctor, hear?"

That was Friday.

She saw the same guard on Monday. He was standing again, with one foot on the road to recovery instead of in the grave.

"You saved my life," he told her.

Karen was glad. Smiled. Time for all good bureaucrats to go to work.

"I had typhoid," he said.

Evidently her five dollars had been enough for him to buy the proper antibiotics. Medical truth? A healthy person won't necessarily die from typhoid. "Only" between 10-30% of cases are fatal. The illness, though, takes four weeks to run its course. The guard would have lost his precious employment. His family would have lost the small security his income bought. Their maddeningly fragile world would have shattered.

The moral of this story? Any amount of charity, in the right hands at the right time, can change a world.

It depends entirely on how you measure that world.

That day, in Sierra Leone, the world for Karen was exactly the size of one man.

Five dollars did the job.

The lights go off in Karen's ground-floor flat in Freetown, Sierra Leone - off for the night. The capital city of one of the poorest countries in the world descends into darkness. We are left with the knowledge that a canteen guard, somewhere in this city, will live to work another day.

And isn't it striking that, even though she is a humanitarian worker, Karen's story of saving a life has nothing to do with her work. It has everything to do with who she is and how she reacted to a situation that presented itself to her.

ACTION — "I DO"

Tom Ahern's story gives us just enough. It doesn't over analyze, it isn't officious and it certainly doesn't procrastinate. It is focused, quite simply, on one thing. On what Karen did. And the impact and change that came from it.

Karen is a real person. But in the story, she could be a metaphor for showing how simple, poignant actions change lives.

Did she go through a moment of *compulsion*? Did she take time and build a longer, deeper *commitment*? Did she have a sense of profound *confidence* that she could do something? She probably had a commitment to her work and a belief that she could make a difference, otherwise she wouldn't have been in Sierra Leone. Maybe it was a moment of *compulsion* that got her into humanitarian work in the first place. Perhaps the *confidence* came from the fact that this was her second trip to Freetown.

At the end of the day, all that fades into the background. For what matters here is that Karen *did* something. She took action!

Karen didn't question whether it might be against the rules to give money to an employee, or what the complexity of the implications could be. She didn't strategize, or pontificate. She didn't position risk management strategies against hedged implementation plans. She didn't ask a committee to meet and provide multiple scenario realities validated by an international and multi-sectorial benchmark. Nor did she refer the issue of the sick guard to an internal review board so that one of their outreach team could be sent case notes in triplicate and organize a peer-review visit of the guard to check on his ongoing medical status at the next scheduled visiting window opportunity.

Karen saw the guard, gave him some money and saved his life. Period.

Action took place. Impact occurred.

Karen didn't have all the information. She didn't know what the guard was suffering from nor how (or indeed if) it would be cured. She gave him five dollars and trusted that Freetown's doctors would do the rest. Isn't it interesting how, in the space of action, doubt often disappears?

She took an *action*. A small *action*. And she let the future write itself.

Compulsion, *commitment* and *confidence* are the first three steps of (me)volution. What Karen does is take us to step four – *action*.

Action manifests *compulsion*, *commitment* and *confidence* into something that other people can see and relate to and creates something that others can engage with. This evolution moves us forward to the next stage of the journey.

At this point, the focus shifts from "I" to "us." We begin to move from the individual to the collective, from a personal to a social expression of our desire for change, and from the vision of one to the potentiality of many.

Put simply, when you actually "do" something, however small, however minor, however apparently unlikely it is to create change, you set in motion a chain reaction that other people can witness and relate to. Others can begin to engage with your action. Motion and impact are created, and that is the beginning of a movement.

THE JOURNEY OTHERS TAKE WITH YOU

The journey with others begins with the formation of a *vision;* building on *values*; thriving on *empowerment* and, if handled well, evolves into the creation of a movement. Martin Luther King created one of the most powerful movements America has ever witnessed. At a time when civil rights and civil liberties signalled upheaval and murderous discord, King created unity and hope articulated by his "I have a dream" speech. In truth, he had a *vision* he called a dream that was formed slowly, over time, as a result of his own personal journey.

It was King's *vision* and tragic death that made him a global icon, but it was his ability to frame and share his *vision* with passion and energy that inspired (and continues to inspire) millions of people. His vision was surely shaped and strengthened over time by the actions he took: attending marches, preaching, listening to travesties of justice or even encountering riot police. These were some of the elements that led him to formulate his vision in a way that could build, galvanize and inspire a movement.

Think about this in a wider context.

As we said earlier, every foundation, non-profit organization, charity or NGO was created by a woman or a man who saw something in the world that they felt needed to change. Their first experiences on the road to that change were likely personal. The (me)volution model shows us that they probably came to the realization that something had to be done, committed to do it and then acquired the confidence to begin it. They experienced the first few steps of (me)volution and then took their first actions. But to get to the point of going beyond themselves required vision - the kind of vision that inspired others to want to join in.

Sam Singh tells us this himself. He explains how his *vision* – of a model for the transformation of rural India – has only taken shape through the work he has done with Pardada Pardidi Educational Society. It has manifested itself in the discovery that when you open a girls' school, you then may need to open a boys' school and that when you've done that, you then may need to also open a hospital. When Sam Singh quit his job at DuPont, he simply wasn't able to formulate his entire *vision*. That was only possible once he started up his first school for girls.

The reality is that, even after going through the first few steps of (me)volution, the ability to articulate the real depth and power of our *vision* is often something that can and will only evolve after taking the first *action*. And that is why vision is the beginning of the *journey others take with you*.

When we share the *vision* that is inside of us, holding in our hands the full scope of what we desire to make happen, that is when passion is released. It is when the downright impossible becomes possible, when boundaries and frontiers of all types are eroded and when people from all backgrounds and creeds are given the opportunity to get behind us, to share in our *vision* and join a movement that they believe in. This is a space where remarkable things happen. This is a space where ordinary people become remarkable. This is the space in which we introduce Brother Kelly Cullen.

BROTHER KELLY'S STORY

told by Kay Sprinkel Grace

Long before his death on November 13, 2010, at the age of 57, words were already being written about a Franciscan Brother named Kelly Cullen who was leading highly visible efforts to provide housing and programs that would lift people out of poverty and addiction in San Francisco: words of praise, words of criticism, and words to help people find the words that would describe him.

He was known for many attributes – enthusiasm, kindness, empathy, seemingly ceaseless energy.

He was called many things – community organizer, ambitious to a fault, challengingly frenetic.

He is remembered for many things – a legacy of inspiring solutions for the issues confronting the poor; a belief that an impoverished neighborhood in San Francisco where many lived from day to day in a haze of drugs and alcohol could become a safe place for families and children – but mostly for his courage and his vision.

For some, he seemed an oxymoron to his calling. As a Franciscan – a follower of St. Francis in the City that carries his name – he was, for many, too much a man of the world. Although he would wear his brown Franciscan robe for special services or meetings, he was equally comfortable in jeans and a sweatshirt or dressed for the opera. He was mad for musical comedy, and would dream up his own words to well-known songs. He and I both shared that passion for musical theatre and I wistfully remember an evening spent listening to the best of the old musicals on vinyl; singing until we could sing no more. His voice was as lyrical as his spirit.

He broke bread with San Francisco's wealthiest, was invited into social circles where others without social standing were ignored. With San Francisco's leaders in the Jewish community he regularly attended classes on the Talmud – relishing the opportunity to swap ideas with the intellectual and business leaders of the city. His vision was part of a hunger he had for life, alongside a curiosity and sense of wonder that were almost childlike in their intensity.

When he achieved unheard of fundraising success for the organization he led, he was criticized publicly for caring more about the money than for the tenants who lived in the housing his organization provided. The critic failed to see that without those funds, the programs would have fallen short of the incredible vision he had.

No visionary can be bold and not draw criticism. Timidity and vision are polar opposites. Brother Kelly had a bold vision, he had swagger, he had a dream, and he had heart.

A wildly capricious, funny, often manic and highly creative thinker, Brother Kelly seized life with a vengeance. To some, he seemed a contradiction of the vows he had taken – he would get in the middle of volatile city squabbles related to urban development and toyed, at one point, with running for Supervisor for the City and County of San Francisco. For someone who had chosen an outwardly simple path for his life, he was immensely complicated.

His vision was unyielding. He was simply intolerant of social injustice. His dream was one of communities where justice is evident in everything from housing to workforce development to family safety to health care. His strong vision was guided by that dream. He gave his dream substance through his decisiveness. Vision is seldom linear, and Brother Kelly embraced many dreams. For him, "impossible" was just an opinion.

The Tenderloin

When Brother Kelly Cullen chose the Tenderloin of San Francisco for his ministry it was a decision that changed the lives of many, including his. The Tenderloin is a conflicted neighborhood of drug addicts, working poor, homeless and immigrant families with few services that sits just blocks away from the high-rise hotels and elegant shopping of San Francisco's Union Square. A business graduate of the University of Washington and the youngest of four rambunctious boys raised in Spokane, he was a seeker from the start. After graduation he spent two years working in a L'Arche community for the handicapped outside Paris. Returning (he never lost his French language or his love of France) he enrolled at the Franciscan Seminary on "Holy Hill" – the cluster of seminaries that lie on the periphery of the University of California at Berkeley known as the Graduate Theological Union.

He joined the Franciscan Order in 1979 and took his lifetime vows in 1982 at St. Boniface Church in the Tenderloin – a church he would be instrumental in saving, not because of the church building, but because of what the church represented to the community.

From his early work with the Tenderloin Neighborhood Recreation Center, where he worked with the city to create an innovative multi-cultural recreation program for children and young adults aged 5 – 20, through his long service as Executive Director of the Tenderloin Neighborhood Development Corporation (TNDC), these people were his. He lived among them: his principal residence was the Franciscan Monastery in the heart of the Tenderloin, but he was also one of the first tenants at TNDC's first building, the Aarti Hotel. He lived for nearly half his life in the Tenderloin, serving his Franciscan commitment while giving many people new hope.

His passion was matched only by his business acumen. When he took over the TNDC, it was struggling financially. With a mission of partnering with the city to create affordable housing for the homeless and working poor, TNDC acquires small hotels and converts them into livable housing with programming that helps people enter the workforce while providing child care and addiction counseling.

When Brother Kelly took charge, TNDC was managing about 575 units of low-cost housing. In 2005, when he stepped down as Executive Director, there were 1,600 units serving nearly 3,000 people. His vision did not flounder when he left: in 2010, there were 2,500 units and it is growing. The current Executive Director, Don Falk, whom Brother Kelly hired in 1993, comments, "Kelly created the infrastructure. The people who have come after him, like me, we're just carrying out the vision that he put into place."

Although he lived in the Franciscan monastery next to St. Boniface Church, his true home was the streets of the Tenderloin. In the city's most transitional neighborhood, he saw only possibilities. From his nearly-forgotten project to restore the neon on old shops, to his widely-applauded success at nearly tripling the number of affordable housing units in the Tenderloin, his often-criticized lack of humility was balanced by a relentless pursuit of his vision.

Brother Kelly was a life eater. He seized life and opportunity together – feeling that one was synonymous with the other. He seemed always to know what he wanted. Seldom have I experienced such determination in a person.

St. Boniface Church

When the Franciscans were told to shut down (and tear down) the Tenderloin's beloved St. Boniface Church because of seismic damage from the 1989 Loma Prieta earthquake, Kelly and his fellow Franciscan friars and the priests said, "No." St. Boniface – whose simple beauty had become an oasis for the poor and the homeless who gathered there each day – simply had to be saved. More than a building, it was a spiritual center. It was a place of profound service to the disconnected and the discontented, to the derelict and the diseased. Its pastor, The Rev. Louis Vitale, OFM, believed, with Brother Kelly, that St. Boniface could be restored. Early estimates exceeded $10 million and the final costs were $12 million – but the efforts of these two Franciscans – one the humble Priest, servant of the poor and fighter of social injustice, the other the bolder Brother who already managed a multi-million dollar corporation that created housing for the poor in the Tenderloin – succeeded. No one believed they could do it. They were the poorest parish in San Francisco, in a part of the community that people avoided.

But this is a story of vision, determination, courage – and joy. It tells how a small team of believers – including Brother Kelly as project manager – managed to raise more than $12 million to completely restore nearly an entire city block of programs that supported ministry to the poor. They retrofit the church, created a new school for the underserved in the community by rebuilding a school that had closed decades before and had more recently been used as a community center, and made improvements to the Monastery.

Brother Kelly first came into my life because of the Tenderloin Neighborhood Development Corporation. It is truly an extraordinary organization that needed some counsel to take it to the next level of donor development, stewardship and fundraising. He sought me out and I had been working with him for more than a year when the St. Boniface project loomed.

It was an urgent need. The "grace" period after the Loma Prieta earthquake was running out, and places where the public gathered needed to be in compliance with tough California law. When the conversation began with the Catholic Archdiocese about the seismic work that needed to be done on St. Boniface, it quickly went awry. The Archdiocese did not support the restoration – suggesting instead that the church be taken down for safety reasons. But Brother Kelly and Father Louie had a different vision: they wanted to restore one of the most beautiful churches in San Francisco and did not want its services to the poor to be interrupted.

They approached me. Did I think we could raise the money? I was captivated by their vision but am a seasoned capital campaigner and wondered whether that much money could be raised. The more I learned about their sense of possibility, the greater mine became. The Franciscans themselves, as an Order, gave the first leadership gift – which they invested wisely with a savvy investment manager who grew the fund by more than 50% by the time the money needed to be used. Another lead gift came from the

Archdiocese. Things were looking hopeful, but it would still be hard to raise the money. Then, a volunteer leader stepped forward – Herman Gallegos, respected retired labor union leader and corporate board member – who began bringing other committed individuals onto a campaign planning committee.

Soon, we were on our way. Brother Kelly named himself as project manager for the campaign (in addition to continuing as Executive Director of TNDC which was growing at a rapid rate) and his vision began inspiring that of others – those same people into whose social circles he had been invited and with whom he studied Talmudic thought.

We also harnessed Fr. Louie's special gifts. He could not have been more different from Br. Kelly – and yet, what a team they made! Father Louie is a shy man whose integrity is so inspiring and his commitment to ending social injustice so strong that people were drawn to his quiet faith and determination. Reluctant to ask for money – the Franciscan tradition does not encourage it – he found his place in the initial year of the campaign as a steward of those who were supporting the church. Handed a phone list on arriving from the next-door monastery each day, he would set to work, calling, engaging and thanking people. Over time, he began to understand how significant this philanthropic outreach was, and stretched it to participate in some of the largest gift solicitations we made – including $1 million from an anonymous donor whose family was well-known to Fr. Louie.

No campaign is without its surprises. Ours was a big one. The Christian Brothers and the Daughters of Charity approached Fr. Louis and Br. Kelly and said they would like to restore the unused school as a Nativity Miguel School – a school where middle school students from the neighborhood could come fully financially supported and, by doing well, ensure their future education through high school and even university. This would add $1 million to the project – school earthquake retrofitting is far more stringent than other public gathering places. But Br. Kelly's vision was steadfast. This was the right thing to do. The Daughters of Charity offered a substantial gift and we felt we could raise the rest.

Putting the dream into the community

Residing at the monastery during that time were several Friars and a priest from Latin America. It turned out they had special gifts, too. But their gifts were not what might be expected: they were masters at creating a robust margarita cocktail and authentic (and tasty) guacamole and salsa. Br. Kelly had an idea. We needed to begin having more cultivation events – we needed to get the community in for a tour and a vision presentation. Why not call our cultivation events "Margaritas at the Monastery?"

Soon this was the hottest invitation in San Francisco. People would call asking how they could be invited. It was written up in several of the most read columns in the San Francisco Chronicle. To this day, people still comment about these events. We would welcome our guests, take them into the church, they would hear from Br. Kelly and Fr. Louie and then go on a tour of the church. Next, they would perhaps hear a short organ recital from one of the Friars and then visit the areas below the church that would become the new men's shelter and kitchen and a restored small theatre for the Tenderloin Opera Company. At the end of the tour they would be rewarded with margaritas (or soft drinks) in the Monastery. The project was rewarded by their interest and eventual financial support.

Br. Kelly never walked or spoke slowly. Impatient, he did not, as the saying goes, "suffer fools gladly." While he gave the love of his faith to those impoverished spirits and people in the Tenderloin, among those with whom he worked and socialized he was quick to speak his mind, shift gears and make changes. If he was going to transform the Tenderloin (which was his vision) he wanted only those around him who were pushing with the same force on the obstacles that rose in front of us.

One day, he handed me an envelope. What was in it became the symbol of our campaign: 12 cents. It had been left in an envelope in the church, and the donor had written on the envelope in perfect Palmer script – the handwriting that all children of the 19th century and into the first decades of the 20th century were taught. He offered his name, his address (homeless) and wrote, "This is all I have. I wish it were more. Thank you."

Brother Kelly's initiative and connections with the media brought us an unheard of endorsement: an editorial in the San Francisco Chronicle on Christmas Eve drawing the community's focus on the "living manger" (yes, real people, real animals) that had been created for a several hour period each evening just before Christmas, citing the vision of the Franciscans and urging public support for this remarkable church.

Gifts to the successful campaign for the restoration of St. Boniface Church and the Franciscan Monastery and the creation of the new De Marillac School exceeded $13 million. In addition to the gifts from the Franciscans and the Archdiocese, they ranged in size from the $1 million anonymous gift to the gift of 12 cents from the homeless man with the perfect handwriting. I attribute this to the inclusive vision that was put forth by Br. Kelly as the visionary and implementer and Fr. Louie as the true shepherd of his parish and a courageous individual who, during our campaign and while in his late 60s, ended up serving a federal prison sentence for protesting against an organization that he felt was unjust.

Brother Kelly saw the campaign through. He proved himself to be both a visionary and a builder, a person capable of engaging disparate constituents into a common desire to transform. One of the larger donors to the campaign, a great admirer of both Br. Kelly and Fr. Louie, spoke for those outside the Tenderloin who stepped forward to make this project happen when he said that it is not possible to have a healthy city when one neighborhood is not as healthy as the rest.

Moving On

Brother Kelly's transformational vision was pushed to the limit by the intensity of this campaign – and the issues related to the restoration which seemed to occur with maddening frequency. The retrofit was much more extensive than anticipated. There were delays. The addition of the school added both costs and time. Towards the end, his frenetic over-driven urge to seize the day began to manifest itself in difficulties with his own life balance. His addiction to his vision had spiralled to a level that neither his work nor his faith could sustain.

In 2005, he stepped aside as Executive Director of TNDC , an organization whose impact in the Tenderloin is without parallel. His incredible impact in support of the homeless, jobless and working poor were life-enhancing for them. He had successfully engaged wealthy individuals committed to the programming of TNDC and their on-going support had ensured several challenge gifts from individuals and foundation funding.

The St. Boniface project was thriving. The DeMarillac School was attracting its own funding and loyal supporters, but all within the context of the transformation that people felt was possible in the Tenderloin.

Discouraged, but not defeated, Br. Kelly set out to quell his demons and get his life back on track. By 2007, he was at a Franciscan retreat center at Old Mission San Luis Rey in Oceanside, on staff. It was no surprise to find him, while there, serving on community boards, teaching and training others and creating events for the retreat center and getting his fair share (again) of publicity.

Italy was his passion. He loved going to Assisi – helping the Franciscans after the devastating earthquake and making pilgrimages whenever possible.

In November, 2010, Br. Kelly took a long-planned trip to Rome to research possible routes for spiritual pilgrimage tours. While on this trip, he went out one evening and never returned. His body was found the next day.

The day before he died, Kelly had sent a number of friends an email stating, in effect, that even if he died that very day, his life would be complete. A long-time colleague found this poem among the collection of many poems he had written:

Absolutely!

I hadn't realized until this night

How very enheartened I am to be returning to Italy

How absolutely full of joy I am!

To be going back...

To hear the musical language

To walk those storied streets

To enter those expansive churches

To look on the inspiration of their beauteous art

To smell and to taste and to touch my senses into the dolce vita

Of every minute in Italia

Yes, to open my eyes upon the rising and the setting colors of that sun and that sky

Is also an opening of soul and spirit and heart to beat palpably

A rush of God into my tiny little steps

Across this amazing planet

A dancing movement encouraged by the life uncovered and lived there

And undeniably woven into me, into my very being

Weeks from now yet I feel it all rising up within me like sap in the springling

Like a bridegroom flying out into daybreak

Like a sunbeam bursting forth into the light

Being light itself in its brightness

How absolutely full am I!

– Kelly Cullen, October 2, 2010

The legacy of vision in philanthropic attainment

What does a person leave behind? What does a Franciscan whose vows were sacred but whose life pushed at the very boundaries of belief leave in this world?

There are buildings that would not be serving the underserved if Br. Kelly had not been there. And there is another gift as well: thousands of lives enriched and stretched because of this complicated person who had chosen a life of simplicity, I suspect, in the hope that it would calm his rambunctious nature. At his memorial service, we were all reconnected with Br. Kelly. The tributes were substantial, the grief unbounded, but the joy triumphed.

One of the many tributes paid to Brother Kelly said:

"No, he wasn't a saint. He wasn't even a monk. Brother Kelly Cullen was a Franciscan friar who followed in the footsteps of St. Francis of Assisi."

"He was driven. He fought for the poor, the oppressed, the homeless, the disadvantaged and the disenfranchised. No one who came into contact with Brother Kelly could resist his charm, his passion, his charismatic personality. This was true whether one was a resident of one of the Tenderloin Neighborhood Development Corporation hotels or a socialite from a wealthy neighborhood. The passion that drove him was contagious, but it was not for his own edification. Rather, it existed for those who had no voice."

"Brother Kelly had power to persuade even the most hardened critics of the homeless in San Francisco because he truly believed that hatred and discrimination did not bring about justice and peace. Throughout his ministry in the Tenderloin, he contended that only through a loving, understanding and compassionate respect for all individuals would our great city live up to the ideals of the name that it bears."

Br. Kelly, who died at the age of 57 in 2010, was a profound visionary who left his work too soon. He was a person of courage, not an easy person to know, but someone whose very channelling of his excessive drive made our world a more vital and interesting place.

He transformed what he touched, and the residual benefits will be felt for generations.

And his vision persists.

VISION – "WE SEE"

The twelve cent envelope. Twelve cents as a contribution to twelve million dollars. Isn't it funny how sometimes it is the smallest things that inspire us the most? This is because we know and we understand that they aren't small at all. Quite the contrary. Putting twelve cents lovingly into an envelope with the name painstakingly written on it was not an action carried out lightly. It was intentional. It was deliberate and it was profound.

This was one homeless and penniless man showing how much the hard work and dedication and *vision* of Brother Kelly mattered; showing that he believed in the church and wanted Brother Kelly's ambitious, maybe even slightly madcap, renovation program to succeed. Though he was on the very margins of the system, this man aligned himself with a friar in jeans who refused the inevitability of the dictats from on high, who put margaritas in monasteries and refused to take the easy way out, all for the good of others.

What we do not know, as the story does not tell us, is whether that homeless man ever knew how much more goodness and philanthropy was inspired by his twelve cents. For one visionary – Brother Kelly – had created another visonary, the homeless man. Together, their vision was shared further. One person has a vision. Another person joins him. And by the actions of both, the vision travels further. It travels out. It begins to journey to places that perhaps neither could have anticipated.

It is during this journey that the passion of the visionary takes hold in the hearts of his or her followers and supporters and it is here that the movement truly takes form. People align with an expressed vision and share it as if it were their own. When the word spreads, the buzz begins.

Yet, even as things get really exciting, certain pitfalls, distractions and challenges are ready to rear their ugly heads.

Imagine this scenario.

A person, we shall call her Mila, lives in a residential suburban community somewhere in North America. Close to her home there is a ravine, where she likes to walk her dog. On a walk one day, she is shocked by the amount of detritus and litter floating down the river. Repulsed, she experiences a moment of *compulsion*. Her *commitment* builds and so does her *confidence*, until one weekend, she pulls out a big garbage bag, puts on her rubber boots and gloves and takes *action* – going down to the river herself to fish out the trash.

A couple of passers-by stop to ask her what she is doing. She shares her revulsion about the state of the river and explains what she is doing. Inspired, they ask if they can help. And so the following day the three of them spend a big part of the day fishing out trash.

The following week, Mila tells this story to a couple of her neighbours, and the next weekend there are seven people fishing out trash.

Mila can see that this is beginning to make a difference. The ravine looks cleaner now than she has ever seen it. And in her own mind, she starts to formulate a vision – one of a river where instead of fishing out trash, you could actually go fishing. At the end of the next day of river clean-up, she shares this vision with the others. It resonates powerfully with them.

Hearing this vision, one of the river collective says that they are going to need more people, and suggests that they create a small non-profit organization which could seek funding to employ someone to help recruit volunteers for future weekend clean-ups along the whole length of the river. One other suggests that they could develop a newsletter and send it to the community, and begin lobbying the local Member of Parliament to put pressure on local industry to stop polluting the river.

So, on another weekend, they meet not at the river, but at a local coffee shop to write up and discuss some papers which say all this and which incorporate a non-profit. It takes the whole day for the collective to agree to the levels of membership that they are going to need, to set up the committees to run all the essential parts of the organization and to define the board structures and terms of reference. They set a calendar for meetings for the Board and for all the committees, and everyone leaves the coffee shop feeling very good about what they have done.

Over the following three weeks, each member of the collective gives more time to the project than ever, yet because of all the work required to manage and administer the organization, they just never seem to have any time to get down to the ravine any more. Litter begins to accumulate again.

This scenario paints a picture that is more common than we would like to admit. When a group of people with a shared vision create an organization to support that vision, a subtle but critical shift happens. The first priority of the organization becomes its own survival, not its ability to deliver impact. This priority shifts from being about the vision, about actually making a difference, to ensuring that the organization has the resources, capacities, processes and energies to be around tomorrow; the theory being that if it doesn't have these things then an organization will not be able to deliver on its mission tomorrow. Yet, this ignores the fact that Mila didn't need any of these things to get the ravine cleaner than she could remember it.

It also ignores the fact that the people who have achieved the most exponential change in the last century or more have done so without cumbersome organizations. In fact, every really transformative movement, from Live Aid to Civil Rights to the anti-Apartheid movement, was not centrally controlled by an organization. It was decentralized and led by passionate change-makers.

Telling the story of Mila is really about sharing a warning. A warning to you as you journey through (me)volution. Be wary of your vision being diluted by the people that you have gathered around you. Not every person who flocks to share your vision, has the power of a homeless person who gives twelve cents and inspires twelve million. They may not share your values.

(me)volution begins with the evolution of the person. It transitions into action and in the process moves the cause from one to many. It transforms the personal drive for change into a public good. Once in the public realm, (me)volution anticipates the formation of a shared vision, common values. When successful, (me)volution manifests in the empowerment of many and the creation of a movement.

VERONICA'S
STORY

told by Jana Ledvinova

For nearly two decades, since the Velvet Revolution swept through old Czechoslovakia, bringing with it both euphoria and Europe-phoria, Veronica had been on the sidelines of society. She was part of a small group of people who did not give up the fight after the wall came down; who didn't subscribe to the new systems set out by civil society that fast-tracked some while leaving others behind. She believed that there was a better world, and a better way out there and it was worth every ounce of energy and passion to try and achieve it.

Veronica was working to develop a culture of philanthropy in a region where civil society had not existed for more than fifty years. Since the fall of communism, she had seen people around her, old school-friends and girlfriends get richer, pursue careers, marry men who had pursued careers, and live lives that were all but unimaginable just a couple of decades previously.

The surge to embrace western-style capitalism caused rifts in society and fostered the opportunity and need for philanthropy. As compassion and values became more and more evident to Veronica, she began to also see people who used to share her world-view change so that she barely recognized them. She was witnessing the birth of a new wave of intolerance and prejudice – often coming from those who had gained the most, and therefore who had the most to offer.

Veronica and Olga were childhood friends. They had grown up together; living in the same block of the Sídlišt Bohnice housing complex in Prague.

Just outside the front door was the concrete staircase where the girls used to spend their evenings in the summer; playing, running, and talking. When Veronica and Olga were fourteen, Olga's family moved from the estate to the town of Kosice, hundreds of miles away down by the Hungarian border. They wrote, faithfully, for months, years even. And then life got in the way.

Veronica was half-way through a glass of something faintly bubbly, struggling with a plate of just defrosted canapés at her 20-year class reunion.

They had both come to the event because the other was going to be there and to see each other for the first time in many years. Veronica had felt real apprehension as she sat on the tram going to the posh hotel hosting the event. But the hugs and the smiles and the joy of seeing Olga again had swept away the fear. Yet, as the evening wore on, Veronica began to wonder if maybe too much water had flowed under the bridge.

"Seriously, after 20 years the first thing she wants to do is play squash!?" Veronica said to herself. "What about coffee? Or dinner? Or drinks? Or a 'come over and meet the kids?' No. She wants to play squash."

It had been a pretty unusual request. Veronica had never set foot on a squash court, but agreed, somewhat puzzled. And so a couple of weeks after their stilted class reunion, she found herself, awkwardly attired and with a borrowed racquet playing alongside her old friend.

From the start, the dynamic was challenging. Veronica chased around the court after the tiny round ball that just wouldn't bounce as high as she thought it should. Olga moved gracefully from one side of the small box to the other…talking all the while about the weekends in her country house, about her two perfect children (7 year-old Peter and 15 year-old Andrea, who were just *so* good at school), about the new car, the wonderful golf course and the country club friends.

Veronica had a different and much simpler life. Her husband wasn't earning country club money. In fact he'd been a house-husband when the kids were younger. Veronica herself was up to her eyeballs, as always, with projects for local NGOs. And far from being idyllic, life was just one long succession of problems. Lots of problems. Many of them tunnels with no apparent light at the end.

But she didn't share them with her old friend.

Veronica was the head of a school in a poor area of Prague. It was a job that not a lot of people wanted but one she relished. The neighbourhood had been a social dumping ground before the revolution and was still the same today. Proof that some things never change, whatever regime you live under.

Recently, the area had seen a huge influx of Roma people – Eastern Europe's *gypsies* – and Veronica had taken it upon herself to integrate many of their children into her school, despite pressures from staff and her management hierarchy to do otherwise. The teachers didn't want the Roma kids, claiming they were dirty and did nothing but disrupt the class and prevent the more talented students from learning.

These, and other similar opinions, were still predominant in the Czech school system even so many years after the fall of communism. Some schools even had separate dining areas for Roma so that the "white kids" wouldn't have to eat lunch with them. Veronica fought this fiercely, and since landing the job had worked diligently to promote equal access to education and tolerance to both children and adults.

She was very proud of what had been achieved in the last few years at the school. Sometimes she had needed incredible determination, patience and self-control, but critical, independent thinking was slowly creeping into the curriculum and classrooms and the nightmare of socialist-style education was becoming a thing of the past. Students in her school no longer had to memorize dogmatic phrases, hold their hands behind their backs or eat and drink on command – all features of pre-1989 Czech education. But she still felt like David fighting Goliath. The status quo doesn't change without pain.

"You know what I am really pleased about?" said Olga, "we have managed to get Andrea into this wonderful private school in Dejvice!"

"It is such a fantastic school. Petr and I toured it last week with the headmistress and were so impressed. The fees are high, but at least there are no *slackers* there - only hard-working, successful people. Andrea will be in very good company." Olga pronounced "slackers" in English.

Veronica paused for a moment. "Slacker" was not a term she was familiar with.

"What is a *slacker*?" she asked.

"Oh, you know, those self-righteous hippies and idealists who have all started up organizations taking good peoples' money to save this or promote equal that or help those who should be helping themselves." She continued, "They are all over the place. It's a good thing Andrea is going to a new school in September, because just last week, she came home telling me that when she gets older she wants to work for this organization that protects animals. I mean, seriously?! She even forced me to buy a yellow flower the other day from this old guy on the street to support some cancer charity. Before the revolution we were all poor and yet we didn't need all these organizations. Why should we need them now, when we are richer and part of Europe?"

Olga grew more and more excited. "The people who run these organizations are always fighting for something, but honestly they can't even look after themselves, let alone other people. They go from paycheck to paycheck, most of them don't even have a car and dress their kids in second-hand clothes."

Veronica missed her next shot and slammed into the wall. But it was not the concrete that hurt.

By the definition Olga gave, Veronica was a *slacker*. A self-righteous idealist. Someone who did not have a car and who dressed her children in second-hand clothes, living paycheck to paycheck: a slacker. She thought of her friends: Vojta, who ran a boxing club for young Roma men giving them a chance to be good at something; Magda, who had fought for three years to create a beautiful green space in the middle of one of Prague's biggest housing estates; Jan, who had just finished raising the money to open the first children's hospice in the country. They were all *slackers* too. And she was proud to be one of them.

Veronica was proud to be a *slacker*.

As Olga and Veronica walked out of the gym together, a family crossed the road in front of them. The mother wore a long black dress, and out of the top of a web of cloth tied around her poked the head of a small child. The father, wearing a backpack, held the hand of a young boy. They walked together.

"Look at them," Olga pointed, with a look of contempt, "and to think that my Andrea wants to turn out like them!"

Veronica began to walk away.

VALUES – "WE BELIEVE"

Private interest versus public good: one of the oldest debates in society.

This eternal question is at the heart of how money flows, how business is organized and is the reason why, for so long, we have had three sectors to the economy. The first sector – business and industry, generates wealth by providing services, creating and selling products. The second sector – the government, regulates the other two to ensure that there is some notion of distribution of wealth and opportunity for most citizens. The third sector – non-profits, address needs that are not met by market forces or government redistribution. The first sector is driven by profit, the second sector by ideology and the third sector by equality, philanthropy and social justice.

But, increasingly, the first sector is realizing that by speaking the language of equity and social justice, it can make more money and thus, more profit. The second sector is financially stretched and relies on everyone else to do its work for it, and the third sector has reached a level of competition where it has, in many cases, become unhealthily focused on collecting money rather than delivering mission. Each of these sectors is changing in profound ways, and as they do so, the notions of collective that they used to incarnate are being profoundly redefined.

What does that mean?

It means that in order to achieve change in a world where the boundaries between companies, charities and government have become almost indistinguishable, we need to engage people not on the basis of sectorial, hierarchical, organizational or institutional attachment, but on the basis of values. The creation of a coherent, values-based movement has become a necessary step in the creation of any transformational change. For today, it is less about effective organizational structure and more about people who believe the same thing joining together under the banner of a vision which inspires them.

Most organizations are based on the tenet of command and control, which comes from a central hub and from the belief that the greatest impact is achieved by top down management. But a command and control structure is not based on values.

Creating a movement for change requires that everyone involved be on the same page. It requires them to have the same understanding, to believe the same things and to be aligned to the same set of values.

In Veronica's story, we meet two childhood friends. Separated after childhood and then reconnected some twenty years later only to find that their common ground has disappeared. Veronica discovers that not only have their points of common experience changed but that they are now on diametrically opposite sides of the philosophical and ideological divide, with different value sets, speaking a very different language.

The last vignette scene in the story illustrates it best. Veronica and Olga see the same thing, yet they react in completely different ways.

As you journey through (me)volution, it is not enough to just share your vision. You must also share your values. They are like the window-display in a shop. They must be transparent, they must shine through. While the name of the shop should convey your vision, the window-display shows off your values. And it is the window-display, even more than the name, that lets people know whether they want to walk through the front door.

It is only when you have clearly shared with the world what you believe in and what you stand for, that you can hope to successfully inspire and recruit the people who will ultimately be responsible for making the change you want to see happen.

MARY KIM'S STORY

told by Simone Joyaux

Inside the envelope: three rather worn single dollar bills.

No note. The return address was that of a parent whose child attended the school - a family with very limited resources.

It was the first time this school had asked for charitable gifts.

I can imagine that if there had been a note, it would have been some form of apology, apologizing for not having more to give. I hear that all the time. What have we done to make others feel they must apologize because a gift "isn't big enough?"

I wonder if this parent felt empowered? Perhaps she wanted to show that – while her gift might not be much compared to others – she did care. And she had the courage to make the gift even though she feared it would be seen as small. It does take courage to make a gift – take action – that one feels might be disparaged. She had the courage and the power to make that gift.

I know that school. I know the director. The values – and hence the organizational culture – are all about empowerment. I suspect the mother felt empowered. She felt empowered despite a society that puts such a high premium on money and the amount of money. But I still worry. She probably thinks $3 doesn't make much difference. And that's a shame. Because when a donor makes a gift - any gift - it makes a difference.

Words matter

"The power of language links people all over the planet: no matter what the tongue, the spoken and written word explains past successes and struggles, defines present perspectives, and expresses future hopes."[4]

---

4 Schultz, Todd. (2009). "The Power of Language," *Muses*, Volume 19, Number 1, College of Arts and Letters at Michigan State University.

This special book has many special words. My first pick would always be "empower." I wonder when the first time was that I thought about empower? I mean thought about it so I knew I was thinking about it...

I probably thought about power first. That would lead me to think about what causes power. In turn, I would then think about lack of power; lack of power links to injustice, which links to inequity. Inequity links to feeling different.

I was raised as an existentialist with an international perspective in the United States, a country that constantly proclaims its exceptionalism and embraces religion far too much. I was taught to welcome pluralism by my French father, who always reminded his family and students: "The important thing is to step out of your linguistic ghetto and become aware that there are people who live, eat, learn, and make love in a medium which is not English."[5]

I use my dad's statement all the time, with my own modification. When I shared this with my life partner Tom, he proclaimed it our family slogan. (By the way, "slogan" comes from the Gaelic "sluaghghairm," used by Scottish clans. It means "war cry." And that's perfect for me.)

My war cry. The war cry of Tom and Simone: "People live, eat, learn, and make love in languages other than English, in colors other than white, and in pairings other than the opposite sex. We are committed to giving voice to and fighting for that beauty."

Of course I would pick the word "empower." Empower is part of my war cry, my most fundamental value and belief: welcoming pluralism because everyone experiences life differently and demanding equity across differences because that's a basic human right.

And empowerment and equity are my great hope for philanthropy – and my biggest disappointment because we're not there yet.

5 Bertsch, Sharon. (1979). "Linguist cites nation's loss," *The State Journal* (Lansing, MI).

Empower. Empower, and then philanthropy becomes a democratizing act.

I'm doing some ranting.

"Philanthropy is commendable, but it must not cause the philanthropist to overlook the circumstances of economic injustice that make philanthropy necessary." (Martin Luther King, Jr., quoted in *Robin Hood Was Right*)

Philanthropy is great. But I want greater. I often criticize philanthropy and the organizations that practice fundraising. Tony Myers once said of me: "The hallmark of your messaging has always been about conversation. And you continue to center your communication and even your 'rants' on the need for conversation of all kinds, but particularly about contentious issues."

Plain and simple: I'm an agitator, asking cage-rattling questions. I challenge accepted wisdom and assumptions. I'm a rabble-rouser. I hope I'm a revolutionary.

Back to my war cry. How do people experience life differently? Through gender and generation, sexual orientation and faith, ethnicity and culture, socioeconomics, and more.

For example: A woman experiences life differently than a man. A lesbian experiences life differently than a straight woman or man. A poor family experiences life differently than an affluent one. In the western world, a white person experiences life differently than a person of color.

But experiencing life differently is about more than differences. Differences actually produce advantages. And what are advantages but privilege. How annoying that we talk so much about disadvantages and disadvantaged people – and don't pay enough attention to the mostly unearned and invisible advantages of the privileged people.

Think about advantage and privilege, and the resulting power. Think about the implications. Visit www.visualthesaurus.com. Search a word. Click on the configurations and links between words. These visual representations stimulate investigation and deeper thought.

> *Advantage: the quality of having a superior or more favorable position.*

And all the changing links? Preference; superiority; leverage; head start.

> *Privilege: a special advantage or immunity or benefit not enjoyed by all.*

And all the changing links on the visual thesaurus? Advantage; right; exclusive right. Privilege produces power.

> *Power: the ability to influence – directs and controls.*

Power; force; might; strength; persuasiveness; freewill; stranglehold. Ain't power grand?

But powerlessness is not so great. What words pop up at www.visualthesaurus.com? Impotence; helplessness; ineffectiveness; uninteresting; unpersuasive.

How about me? What advantages – privilege – do I have? I'm a white, heterosexual, well-educated, affluent woman. All of these are advantages in many countries – all, that is, except for my gender. And most of my advantages – certainly race / ethnicity and sexual orientation – are unearned. I was born white and heterosexual. My parents financed my education. My education and race helped me get good jobs.

How about you? What advantages do you have? Who has the privilege in your society – unearned and too often invisible?

Now think about the status quo. You know, the existing state of affairs. The circum-stances that just make things the way they are. Synonyms like: environment, equilib-rium, acceptance. And the opposite, exclusion. There's great motivation to maintain the status quo. There's powerful incentive to exclude differences that threaten equilibrium. And there's so much inertia to change.

Are you wondering why I'm doing all this ranting about privilege and power?

Think about it. What messages do most non-profits send in the way they carry out their activities and engage in philanthropy? Is the non-profit sector using and reinforcing the status quo? Sure it is. Listen to the way charities and foundations talk about finding people of influence and affluence for their boards. Listen to the consultants who say, "Oh my, you don't have the right board members with enough connections to raise lots of money." The business of changing the world has been reduced, too often, to a financial transaction.

It has become too much about money and not enough about people. It is often so much about privilege and power - about power *not* empowerment.

Is the non-profit sector using and reinforcing the status quo? Yes indeed. It needs money for all of its good missions. Does it use privilege and power to do its work? Yes. I call this philanthropy's moral dilemma.[6]

Colleagues at a recent conference said to me: "Our job is to take money from the rich and give it to the poor. We should use the rich that way." Okay. I agree that non-profits need to find people who care about their causes and ask them for gifts. And hopefully some – even many – of those donors are able to invest gifts that produce significant resources for the cause.

Some colleagues at this same conference said that my concept of philanthropy's moral dilemma was an issue in the USA, not a global issue. Now anyone who knows me knows that I have big issues with the USA - that I believe the U.S. is an arrogant, imperialistic, and hegemonic country. Nonetheless, the USA is not the only place where the status quo is embraced and the haves and have-nots get further and further apart.

6 Philanthropy's moral dilemma: privilege, power, reinforcing the status quo. Read more about this concept in *Keep Your Donors*.

There's enormous poverty and gigantic wealth in other countries, too. The disparity is stunning and, may I say, vicious. The status quo is the status quo. Privilege and power are held by far too few hands. And you know what all this really means? Injustice. Social injustice.

> *"Give a man a fish and you feed him for a day. Teach him how to fish and you feed him for a lifetime."* **- Lao Tzu**

But there's something missing from that proverb. Unless the man (or woman) has a place on the river to fish from, learning to fish is useless. Getting a place on the river is social justice. Giving money to an organization that's fighting to get spots on the river for those who fish – that's social justice.

Traditionally, the dominant norm in many societies is distributing fish to the hungry and even providing employment training programs to develop fishing skills. But sharing places on the river...that may upset the status quo. That kind of inclusion – equity – may threaten the privileged.

Besides the addition to Lao Tzu's proverb, here's another story that illustrates the difference between the two.

Imagine that you're walking along a riverbank. Suddenly you notice babies floating down the river, drowning. You wade into the river and rescue them, but there are still more, so many. Soon, you see another person walking along the riverbank. You call out to her, "Come and help me save the babies who are drowning in the river." But she rushes by, saying, "I'm going to the head of the river to figure out who is throwing them in and stop them." "Rescuing the babies" is the traditional and dominant approach that the third sector takes to problems in society, both locally and globally.

Going to the head of the river to fix the root cause is less common and often controversial. Why controversial? Because social justice questions privilege and the privileged. It seeks to overturn the status quo and make social change. And social change? Well, that alters the fabric of society.

It is true, both approaches matter. The choice is not either/or.

We need to teach people to fish and rescue the babies in the river. But we also need to make places on the river for the fishermen and women. And we need to go to the head of the river and stop the system that throws babies in.

But I'm frustrated that social change philanthropy is not well enough known in our societies. That's another element of what I see as philanthropy's moral dilemma, this lack of awareness.

I expect the non-profit sector to recognize the interconnected machinations of privilege, power, status quo, and philanthropy. I expect all non-profit organizations to question this, to challenge assumptions and ask cage-rattling questions and engage in meaningful conversation. Let's not just do what's always been done.

I'm angry that there isn't enough money given to social change philanthropy worldwide, to solve the root causes of problems. Bottom line: The less social justice we have, the more philanthropy we need. We need more philanthropy to compensate because we never give enough to actually make social change. And I think that's because true social change and social justice threaten our own unearned and invisible privilege – along with our earned privilege.

I suppose that's why the book *Robin Hood Was Right* resonates so much with me. The subtitle is *A Guide to Giving Your Money for Social Change*. In this book I encountered words that really spoke truth to power, and promoted philanthropy as empowerment: empowering activism, empowering volunteer time and giving money, empowering those who typically don't have power. It also discusses empowering people to demand power because it's never freely given (thank you Frederick Douglass[7]), building solidarity and maybe stimulating people with power (produced by privilege, most of which is unearned and invisible) to question their own privilege and the resulting power.

I'm a fundraiser. And fundraisers talk about the transformative power of giving. We know that giving can transform the life of the donor because donors tell us that. And as donors ourselves, fundraisers experience transformation.

Fundraisers and organizations and donors talk about the transformative power of a gift. A gift that makes such a big difference that life changes, the planets realign. And that's great.

But I wonder if everyone – the fundraisers, organizations, and donors – is mostly talking about really big money. I wonder how many are talking about $3 gifts or gifts from the clients who cannot afford to pay for the service but find money for a charitable contribution.

Honestly, I wonder how often fundraisers and organizations talk about the transformative gifts of people who are empowered to give no matter their resources. I wonder how many fundraisers and organizations honor those donors and admire their empowerment. I wonder how many fundraisers and organizations welcome and promote philanthropy as an empowering and democratizing act.

---

7 Frederick Douglass, 19th century American abolitionist, women's suffragist, orator, author, and reformer, once said: "If there is no struggle there is no progress. Those who profess to favor freedom and yet deprecate agitation are men who want crops without plowing up the ground, they want rain without thunder and lightening...This struggle may be a moral one, or it may be a physical one, and it may be both moral and physical, but it must be a struggle. Power concedes nothing without a demand. It never did and it never will."

Imagine philanthropy designed to empower – and not just for Bill and Melinda, as I affectionately refer to the Gates. And rest assured, Bill and Melinda are referred to in every country in the world, not just in the USA. Their kind of money, their foundation, grabs attention everywhere.

I always say that philanthropy has existed ever since the beginning of time, with the first Homo Sapiens in caves. People took the responsibility and the power to help each other, to make a difference, to make change. And just as philanthropy has existed since the beginning of time, so have privilege and its resulting power.

Just as everyone admires Bill and Melinda Gates, I want everyone to admire the mother who gave $3. I want everyone to admire people who are not as famous as Gandhi or Buddha or Wangari Maathai or Aung Sang Suu Kyi or Muhammad Yunus.

I expect (not just want, but expect) people to understand that there are two classes of philanthropy – traditional and progressive – just like there are two classes of people (haves and have-nots).

I hope donors of affluence admire the donors of other-sized gifts because a *major* gift is determined by the donor, not someone else.

I want fundraisers and organizations to use philanthropy as an empowerment strategy, not just a financing mission strategy. Rest assured, I'm neither naïve nor contemptuous.

"Not what you possess but what you do with what you have, determines your true worth." - **Thomas Carlyle**

I know that non-profit organizations need money to do their good work. I know that they need all kinds of gifts, all sizes of gifts. Effective organizations focus on return on investment. And it's unlikely that an NGO can fulfill its mission with tons of gifts of $3 only.

I honor the choices that donors make when they give time or money. I respect fundraisers who work for causes that make their hearts sing. All I ask is more awareness within this, the third sector. I do expect world-changers to expand their knowledge and take the risk to ask cage-rattling questions. I trust that society will learn to question the status quo and privilege and power.

And I believe that part of the value and the intent of changing the world is not to reinforce the status quo but rather to challenge the status quo and promote real social change.

"Let every soul look upon the morrow for the deed it has performed." - Qur'an, 59:18

Remember the story of the school, the parent, and her $3 gift? Here's another story from that same school.

One day, the school director was visiting with a parent. The director brought a luscious dessert to enjoy, tres leches cake. The delighted parent enjoyed this traditional dessert immensely, saying, "I used to bake this a lot, but not anymore."

"Why no longer?" asked the director. And the parent responded, "Because it requires 45 minutes of baking and I don't want the oven on that long. The oven uses too much energy and that's too expensive."

This same parent sent a $50 gift to the school shortly thereafter. She chose to give.

"The true meaning of life is to plant trees under whose shade you do not expect to sit." - Nelson Henderson

Meet Mary-Kim

"Why are you so hell-bent on fixing everything?" A former co-worker asked Mary-Kim that question. And she was still flabbergasted weeks later telling me the story.

"But what else is there?" Mary-Kim said to me. "What will I do with my life? Why get up in the morning if I don't think I can make something better? Why have children or work or look to the future? What would propel you if you didn't think you could make something better?

"How could this person ask 'why are you so hell-bent on fixing everything?'"

"Why bother to live with that attitude?" Mary-Kim mused. "You have to engage because there's all this work to do."

Mary-Kim and I were sharing a yummy dinner after a board meeting of the Women's Fund of Rhode Island. Mary-Kim was the chair back then; I'm the founder and first board chair. As always, our conversation was far ranging. We talk politics and privilege. We talk about life-partners and families and working women. We talk leadership and change and even revolution.

That evening, I told Mary-Kim about this book and my chapter about the word "empower." I asked about her bequest to the Women's Fund. She shared her donor story with me, and she answered the challenge from her former co-worker. It wasn't a question to learn and understand. His "why bother" was an aggressive and defiant challenge.

Mary-Kim is a thirty-something feminist, mother of Zooey and William and life-partner to Matt. At the time of this story, she was also Executive Director of a Rhode Island non-profit, a poet, a respected and admired colleague and bequest donor to the Women's Fund.

I asked why she made that bequest. Her first response: "I believe in the organization. I believe in modeling behavior for others. And a bequest was an easy, easy way to demonstrate my commitment. What I can do right now depends upon my cash flow. But I wanted to reserve money right now for the future. Giving to the Women's Fund – reserving part of my estate for the Women's Fund – is important as I move through my life. Giving a bequest isn't for old people. It's for me now. And it's for my children."

I kept asking. We kept talking.

"It's important to articulate one's personal values. My bequest reflects my values," said Mary-Kim. And as is the case with discussions about the Women's Fund, social justice came into the conversation very early. "Social change is a long-term proposition," observed Mary-Kim. "Yet we too often think short-term and immediate gratification. I made a long-term commitment – the bequest – in recognition of the longer term.

"We don't know what the change will produce – so we keep doing it and hope that, eventually, there will be a positive outcome. Change – the real thing – won't happen in my lifetime. But my bequest will help the process of change." And then Mary-Kim talked about planting trees even though she'd never enjoy their shade.

That's powerful. Investing in the future that you know you will not experience. But Mary-Kim's children and grandchildren will experience that future. So will my nieces and nephews. And equally important, so will all the children in all the possible futures.

"If I have it or might have it," said Mary-Kim, "why not claim it now?" Note her phrase: claim it. Claim it. She claimed future money for the future. She claimed a portion of her children's inheritance to make change for their future.

Say it loud. Scream it from the street corners and riverbeds. "I claim my power. Join me and claim yours. And together, we will make a difference." Mary-Kim claimed her power. Just like the two women from the school. Just like all the many, many people who give their time and money around the world.

By now, Mary-Kim and I were closing in on dessert. The insights grew deeper and deeper.

I asked Mary-Kim what "empower" means to her as a donor.

She responded that giving was a benefit to her personally. "It's my chance to make a public statement about what I believe in. And I trust that the organization will do what I think should be done and that I'm part of that action." That's empowerment.

She talked about empowering her daughter, Zooey by helping to fill up her toolkit to face the challenges in her life as a woman. She talked about empowering William to see his mother and father in different roles. Mary-Kim talked about empowering the Women's Fund to do its work, which in turn would empower Zooey and William, and has empowered Mary-Kim. What a lovely virtuous circle is this philanthropy, eh?

And then the conversation turned to privilege and power.

"There are certain ways that I have power," said Mary-Kim. "People who have the ability to act and have the resources to do so have a responsibility to do it if they see things that need to change. I'm aware of the relative power that I have, especially compared to situations where I don't have power. Every time I experience my own privilege, I channel it because the value of my action is urgent and imperative. If I can't use whatever relative power I have to address situations that need to be addressed, what's the use of having any power?"

Now there's a truth. As Mary-Kim asked, "If a person doesn't use the power s/he has..." And then she stopped talking. We both just looked at each other. We were back to claiming one's power, despite its limitations or because of them.

Mary-Kim started up again. "It's a choice. There are so many choices that we do *not* have. There's so little power in certain situations. So we choose. We empower ourselves to choose when we can. Or else we don't, and that's too bad. It's more meaningful and potentially impactful to choose to exercise the power we have."

"I don't have that much money. But what money I have, I have choices about. For me, life is about exercising the limited or limitless choices one has." And then she told me about the question her former co-worker asked: "Why are you so hell-bent on fixing everything? Why bother?"

"Because, something different than the norm creates more possibility," said Mary-Kim.

Something different than the norm. Beyond the status quo. Creating possibilities. Questioning and learning and demanding change makes us human – and that's the value we add to the world, I think. Is it not the great pride of humanity to strive for better? Making meaning is essential to human life. And we can't make meaning if we don't empower ourselves.

Each day different people wake up and experience life differently. In every community, some change about something would make a healthier place to live.

"Anything that encourages or provides access to a different way of thinking adds value. And if there's one different way, then there are more different ways. There has to be some value in the difference. That difference has to mean something. It's the thread of history, one point leading to another point. It's mostly subtle and incremental changes but sometimes it is revolutionary changes. My mother had limited choices," said Mary-Kim. "I have more choices. And Zooey and William must have even more choices."

And finally, Mary-Kim mused, "How sad not to feel like an actor, an agent of something in one's own life and in one's own world.'"

Empower those who care to give. Maybe the gift will fight global warming or ensure after-school programs for troubled youth or expand the museum's collection.

Empower those who believe in your cause to invest in that cause. Maybe the contribution will fund medical research or a free clinic for families or continue the distinction of an educational institution.

Empower others to fulfill their own aspirations. Help all those you touch give to what they care most about.

Empower people to choose, to claim their own voices and actions, no matter the limits.

Empower individuals.

Empower organizations.

Empower yourself to raise challenging questions.

Empower all of us to belong.

EMPOWERMENT – "WE BUILD"

Let us return, for a moment, to Mila and her ravine cleaning endeavours. Let's imagine that after spending a whole load of time writing processes and terms of reference and other such assorted, crucially important things, Mila and her cohort finally get back to cleaning up the ravine and one of two scenarios plays out.

Scenario 1:

The word spreads around the community that people are giving up time to clean the ravine. Mila contacts local media and encourages everyone in the community to take an old plastic bag and come out for a couple of hours on the weekend to be part of the clean up. It has a spontaneous, fun feel to it, and over time there is a growing group of people who like to come down to the ravine, who meet new friends and who feel that they are part of something that is making a difference. The organization starts providing food and soon there is a big community picnic every Sunday with people who have never been to the ravine popping in to see what the fuss is about. A few businesses contact the organization and ask what they can do, some individuals also come with suggestions of other initiatives that can be run, others want to donate money, the politicians want to be involved and get told that they can develop legislation to better protect it from pollution. The ravine is cleaner than it has ever been and the community is re-engaged with its local environment.

Scenario 2:

The organization runs a campaign to sign people up to be part of scheduled ravine-cleaning teams that go out at pre-defined times. When you sign up, which you can do online or by responding to their mailings, you are given a number and told to report to a certain address at a certain time to receive your standardized and pre-strengthened bags and a health and safety training session on the importance of not falling into the water. Strong shoes or rubber boots are obligatory and children under the age of twelve are not allowed, for insurance reasons. Volunteer cleaners are entered into a database and sent a mailing that contains a brief thank you while asking for money to support the organization in its great work to clean out the ravine. Reports are issued and sent to local policymakers showing that the progress of the ravine cleaning initiative has reached set benchmarked targets and that this area should be recognized as a priority local environment community measure under local authority target setting. To maintain volunteer numbers in an environment where it is so difficult to find and keep good volunteers, the organization increases its spend on marketing for volunteer recruitment and projects cutting 20% of the scheduled ravine-cleaning team activity slots for the following financial year. The ravine is still full of trash. And no-one in the community cares.

It's almost comical, isn't it?

Yet, many non-profits, at some point in their development, end up drifting into scenario two. And we can name more than a few who have nigh on perfected the art of taking the satisfaction out of doing good! Most organizations do not galvanize movements for this simple reason – that instead of seeking to facilitate a fun, engaging and rewarding environment where change can happen, they prefer to command and control, optimize and manage. And let's face it, who wants to join a bunch of managers?

The key thing to realize is that the change-makers who are credited with building or leading movements to effect change have not actually built the movements. They have created the environment where the movement can grow. They have guided it, they have led it. But more than anything, through their leadership and inspiration, they have empowered it.

Iconic change-makers – from Gandhi to Mandela, from Lech Walesa to Ang San Suu Kyi - have all led change through the empowerment of others.

The word *empower* itself is fascinating. It literally means, "giving power to others." But while that is all well and good, if you have the power and you give it to others, what should they do with it? What do you expect them to do with it?

This is the crunch.

And as we journey towards the culmination of (me)volution we are going to be faced with this crunch. For empowerment is the ultimate step in your journey.

To get real change to happen, as we have seen, we need a clear *vision* and a common sense of *values* and purpose. Then the people who have joined us need to know what they are supposed to be doing. They need to know that they have the tools, or that the tools will be provided for them, to go forward and make change.

One of our favourite examples of empowerment happened during the first Obama election campaign of 2008. The Obama team set out a clear vision – a vision that was simple enough to be consensual yet powerful at the same time – and then crucially, they empowered people with the tools to swarm together and get him elected. Obama didn't get himself elected. The movement did. He just held the fort and ran a solid campaign so that Americans wouldn't have too many reasons to NOT elect him.

Achieving political change used to be solely about money. The party with the most money won elections. But Obama had less money than the Republicans when he started the campaign. Much less. What Obama (or rather Chris Hughes, the founder of Facebook and the brains behind the Obama online communities) understood, was that if you could share a vision and values in a powerful enough way then your real supporters would not only self-identify, they would flock to the cause. He understood the concept of (me)volution. He also understood that if he could find out from these supporters what tools they needed to help achieve the vision, and then provide them, that they would do the work.

At one point during the campaign, Obama supporters wanted to be able to call up the swing voters in their local area, but didn't know who to call. This information was held in difficult to access centralized databases at Obama headquarters. So, the Obama team listened to their supporters, and built a link to the database for campaigners.

But they didn't stop there.

They also built an online integrated calling tool so that calls could be made, and information recorded, in one place. That way, all the volunteers knew what was going on and could make the right calls at the right time.

But they didn't stop there.

They also ran massive teleconferences to train campaigners in how to use the system, and then held their hands when they needed to get questions asked.

What was the impact?

Millions of calls made.

Of course, history has taught us to look back on this particular political campaign as a defining moment – the first time where mass mobilization was really harnessed and unleashed in the political sphere.

Whether this historical interpretation is entirely true or not, what *is* for sure is that the growth of the internet, in social marketing and in remote working techniques formed a base on which the Obama team were able to build their empowerment strategy. And this strategy, and the tools that were developed as a result of it, did indeed empower hundreds of thousands of Democrat activists and community mobilizers to go out and get Obama elected. And from that, we can learn about the impact of empowering others to help you realize your vision.

When a change-maker reaches this stage in (me)volution, their journey, vision and (oddly enough) their role has been well and truly transformed. They are now leaders and ambassadors – still sharing the vision and values, but focused on really listening to those who have joined them, and to provide them with the tools that *they* need to deliver the change.

It adds a level of complexity for us as (me)volution change-makers. By the time we get to this stage, we will surely still, at some level, feel the compulsion that you felt back at the beginning of the process. Yet you will have to articulate it with the reality that the change is being mostly driven and achieved by others. You will now be making your dream happen, by the most wonderful of paradoxes, not by doing it, but by empowering others to do it for you – for THEY will build it, not you.

A word of caution: herein lies another pitfall. It is called "founders' syndrome."

It happens to the most gifted activists. It happens to the most passionate advocates and change makers. They go through (me)volution, creating an inspiring vision, drawing in like-valued people, and then for some reason the entire process grounds to a halt.

What happens is that these gifted and talented and even inspiring change-makers refuse to empower. They refuse to give up control. They don't give up their creation for others to own, to run with and to build. And as a result, they kill the feeling of ownership that like-valued people crave in order to adopt a mission that speaks to them. Founders' syndrome is a disease that kills change quicker than any other that we can think of.

Why does this happen?

We broached this subject early in the book when we talked about the role of *confidence*. We talked about fear stalling progress. We talked about how fear can cramp our learning, paralyze our thinking, destroy trust and cause us to avoid risk and hunker down and move from a world of expanding external focus, to inward paralysis.

Beware of founders' syndrome. It kills change.

Behold *empowerment*. It creates change.

In her chapter, Simone posed a question. An eternal and profound question.

Who do you want to be – the swimmer plucking the babies from a fast-moving river, or the person who goes to the mouth of the river to stop babies being thrown in the water in the first place?

The first, or the second. Or maybe a bit of both?

In many cases, we are called to deal with the symptoms, rather than attack the root of a problem. The symptoms are more obvious and easier to address, for sure. The root cause of a problem is usually less obvious, more difficult to determine and even more challenging to address. Solving it takes more time and is more difficult to mobilize.

So where will you put *your* focus? Where will you put the majority of *your* energies? Will you embrace the cause and remove the problem, rather than just reducing the impact of what the problem causes?

Sam Singh, Ken Shipley and Noerine Kaleeba all give us examples of how you can do both. How you can ease the pain, whilst at the same time focussing on solving the problem. In Uganda, Noerine has created the organization that distributes the drugs that allow hundreds of thousands of people to stay alive. But she is also spending a large part of her life flying around the world and meeting with powerful leaders to try and get the resources to Africa to actually turn the tide on this epidemic.

Sam Singh went to the root cause of poverty – lack of education – and is trying to solve the problem. Will either Sam or Noerine solve the issues overnight? No, they absolutely won't. But the more they can build support, the more they can empower others and grow the movement, the more voice they will have and the more change they can effect.

Changing the world is not only about making ourselves feel better because we are doing something good. At the end of the day, if (to misquote Simone) we are just teaching people to fish without redistributing fishing access rights are we just perpetuating the problem?

* * *

With luck, some things in this book will have resonated with you. Hopefully you have remembered or reconnected with a moment, or maybe several moments, of compulsion. Now, maybe you are thinking about what you could do with that compulsion and how you might follow up on it.

We hope you feel inspired by the stories and emboldened by the (me)volution model so that you know that you are not alone in this journey. By reading this book you should have a better understanding of what others have gone through, and of the steps others have taken as they made their way towards the changes that they made in the world. Are you inspired to make changes in your world and in the world of those around you?

We are writing this book, because we believe that more people than ever before have the ability, the potential and the ideas to make real change. But for whatever reason, they haven't got around to it yet. We hope that understanding the journey and seeing examples of the steps others have taken, will solidify a piece of valuable knowledge: that all change begins by taking one, small, first step. No status quo has ever been broken, no change has ever occurred, without someone taking some kind of action.

Solving the problems that face our societies around the world is challenging. It doesn't happen overnight. It takes commitment, dedication, and it takes time and money. But once the problem has been solved, it has been solved.

A few years ago, after the fall of the Soviet Union, a plethora of charities were set up to deal with the inhumane conditions that orphans in Romania were living under. Most of them built orphanages, looked after kids, and then as the governments and European Union began to improve the structural provision of healthcare and support to orphans, they diversified into other things, widening their mission, or increasing their reach to deal with adults as well as non-orphaned children.

One small French charity called SERA did the opposite.

SERA was created to deal with the lack of provision of adequate care for orphans in one area of Romania. It raised money, built orphanages, lobbied politicians, and got the problem solved. And then it closed its doors. Because the change it had sought to make had happened. The problem no longer existed. It had achieved the change it was set up to achieve.

Pause for a moment. Think about the real question here. What are we actually going to empower people to do? And is that the *best* way to achieve the change we want to achieve?

And realize that your (me)volution journey doesn't necessarily require you to build an organization that will grow into a megalithic structure that will outlive you. You can help create something to solve a problem, solve that problem, then close up shop and go back and have a whole new (me)volution journey. For you will have achieved change. You will have achieved transformation – at whatever level and whatever scope you decide.

Now isn't that an exciting prospect?!

DAVID SERRA'S STORY

told by Jon Duschinsky

"We sometimes think that poverty is only being hungry, naked and homeless. The poverty of being unwanted, unloved and uncared for is the greatest poverty" - **Mother Teresa of Calcutta**

The snow had not yet begun to fall, but there was a definite chill in the air. It was late in October, and the streetcar rails shone like landing lights in the headlamps of rush-hour traffic.

Around the entrance to the arts centre, a crowd was forming. Long coats and scarves over suits and dresses. Waiting for friends or loved ones. Talking. Smoking. Enjoying the revitalizing feeling of the sharp air. Everyone impeccably dressed. Waiting for the bell to ring.

David and his wife had almost perfect seats. They could see the whole stage.

Music stands were everywhere the eye could see. The stage was simply full of them. More than two hundred and fifty, each one perfectly laid out in front of a pair of chairs. The sort of chairs that you find in old hotel banqueting suites – the ones they put faded white covers over to add decorum.

As the audience took their seats and the hum in the auditorium increased, David felt a rush of excitement. Had it really been almost 35 years? That long since he first joined the movement? It certainly didn't feel like a *movement* then, not in the sense that it was now. It felt more like a family – a group of friends spending time, learning, playing, having fun. Back then, who would have imagined what it would be today? Who would have imagined that he would be here, three decades later and three thousand miles away in this most prestigious Canadian concert hall, reconnecting with this *movement* that brought him so much joy and happiness as a child?

The lights dimmed. And more than two hundred players of the Simon Bolivar Orchestra entered the stage, instruments in hand and smiles beaming across their young, impassioned faces. After a joyous musical cacophony of tuning, and applause to greet the conductor, there was silence. David held his breath.

While David Serra holds his breath, let us discover more about him. To begin with, a disclaimer: this is not David's story. He is far too modest to allow anyone to tell it. But it is a story in which he has played a part. To be honest, this is not really any one person's story, but more a story about people - about humanity. About human beings coming together and creating movements that - like waves - spread goodness and greatness far and wide. David is our guide in this story. He will help us discover some of the protagonists who, together, built the *movement* he refers to so fondly. He will help us understand how this *movement* produced a transformation of a sort that no-one could have imagined three decades previously.

Today, David is a father, a business owner and a citizen of the city of Toronto, Canada. He is a happy, successful man. But the thing he is most proud of – what he calls "his greatest accomplishment" is something that he did many, many years ago.

David was a nine year-old schoolboy in Carona, Venezuela back on the day in 1975 when his journey began. Two music teachers came, pretty much unannounced, into his class with violins and began to play. David sat back in his chair, enjoying the change in rhythm from the traditional school day, and drifted with the beautiful sounds coming from these small pieces of fragile wood. He watched as the bow swayed back and forth over the strings, with sometimes short punching movements and other times long, graceful waves. He was enchanted, his notion of time lost for the duration of the music. The beginning of the journey.

The teachers came to the end of the recital and put down their bows, and David and his classmates erupted in excited applause. What happened next was an even greater surprise. The teachers turned to the class and asked who wanted to learn to play an instrument. David's hand shot up (as did more than half the hands in the room) in one of those "reaching for the skies, please look at me, please choose me, me, me" moments when your arm feels it might actually detach itself from the shoulder.

A few days later, he was standing in a room at the "Casa Villa Cultura" in Carona, with the same two music teachers and those classmates who had put their hands up. The room was filled, absolutely crammed with musical instruments of all possible types and shapes, almost all of which looked entirely foreign to David. He recognized some drums, and what looked like a bigger version of the violin that the teacher had played in the classroom, but he had no idea about the others. But he couldn't take his eyes off of them, their sparkling black, gold or shiny wood pulling him in like a vortex. He faintly heard one of the teachers speaking, "We will learn how to play these beautiful musical instruments. For fun. No-one will force you to learn, to practice, or to come here. We will play together, learn together and have fun together. You will begin to master your instru-ment, or maybe you will decide it is not for you and stop. That is fine too. The important thing is to enjoy the music, enjoy each other and learn together. Now, walk around the room and see which instrument is going to be yours."

David followed his classmates, slowly approaching an instrument, as if afraid of it, touching, wondering what it did, plucking a string here, banging a cymbal or pressing a key there. Gathering his courage, he walked over to an instrument that was sitting on its own and didn't seem to be attracting a lot of attention. It looked like a black tube with most wonderful shiny silver pieces of metal. It had a hole in one end and a wedge-like taper at the other. He reached out and touched it.

"That is an oboe, young man." David turned to see the teacher leaning over him. "They are difficult instruments to play, but if you like it I'm sure we can do something for you. Pick it up, hold it, see if it speaks to you and if you would like to go home with it and care for it as if it were your most precious toy."

David walked home that evening with "his" oboe, cradling the heavy case in both hands as if it were a fragile egg that he wanted to protect with all his might. When he opened the door, the first thing he did, before greeting his parents or even sharing his incredible day with them, was to take his oboe up and hide it in the closet away from prying eyes or indelicate fingers. Taking care of it, as if it was indeed the greatest gift he had ever received.

The two music teachers didn't just visit David's school. They went all over town, to every school and youth club, sharing their joy of music. Soon four of David's seven brothers had met them, been inspired by them and had brought home musical instruments that they were spending their free time learning, playing and discovering. The flute, the violin, and oboe all played together, creating a joyous cacophony in the Serra's small home.

Every day, from 4pm to 9pm, David and his brothers would willingly attend orchestra rehearsals. There, they learned music. They learned notes and chords and technique and musical theory and musical history. They learned discipline. They learned respect. In David's own words, "It was like a family - children from high-class and low-class families joining together, playing together. We didn't worry about where other kids came from, which part of town they lived in, or how they were dressed. We only worried about how well they played. People used to stop me in the street and say, 'hey, I've heard you're in the orchestra!' I felt such a feeling of recognition, of belonging."

So, where did these two magical, almost Pied Piper-ish music teachers come from to infect a community with music and impact it in such a powerful way?

The teachers were two of the founders of the *movement* David referred to earlier, a *movement* known today as El Sistema. In more official terms, it is called the Fundacion des Estado para el Sistema Nacional de les Orquestas Juveniles e Infantiles de Venezuela. From a more pragmatic viewpoint, it is Venezuela's unique and quite incredible national system of free music education that aims to bring the transformative power of music to children.

Started in 1975 by Dr José Antonio Abreu, El Sistema – literally, "the system" has gone from being one man's vision to being the most successful musical youth program in the world. Targeting at-risk children and young adults from ages 2 to 20, the El Sistema movement has created over 300 youth orchestras in Venezuela, helping more than one million children out of poverty and on to a brighter future. El Sistema is truly a movement that has achieved, and continues to achieve, transformative change.

Dr José Abreu is the man behind this phenomenon. Despite receiving a doctorate in economics, he is one of the greatest conductors and musicians that South America has ever produced. He has dedicated his rich and varied life to the vision that an orchestra is an ideal for society - "it is the only community that comes together with the fundamental objective of agreeing with itself."

His vision was that every child should have the opportunity to be exposed to the orchestral community from as early an age as possible. By doing this, he believed, it would be possible to create a generation of more rounded human beings, capable of accessing and channeling their emotions, grounded in fundamental values and with a greater understanding of the principles of tolerance, discipline and respect. These children would become adults that could work their way out of poverty and into opportunity, children who would be better equipped to build stronger and fairer societies for the good of all.

"Music becomes a source for developing the dimensions of a human being," said José Antonio Abreu in his 2009 acceptance speech of the prestigious TED Prize, "thus elevating the spirit, enabling a sense of commitment, responsibility, generosity and dedication to others. All this leads to the development of self-esteem and confidence. The child becomes a role model for his parents, and this is very important for the poor child. Once the child discovers he is important for his family, he begins to seek new ways of improving himself and hopes better for himself and his community. From the minute a child is taught to play an instrument, he is no longer poor! He is a child in progress, hoping for social and economic improvements for his own family, and in turn encouraging the most vulnerable strata of the Venezuelan population...to embrace new dreams and new goals."

Classical music as a tool for transformational change

Violins against violence.

Flutes for freedom.

Trumpets teaching tolerance.

Margaret Mead talks about the power of a small group of determined people to bring real change, as is the example of José Antonio Abreu. Today, more than a million children, teenagers and adults – including 47 year-old David Serra – owe a big part of their lives to José and his vision. Most of them were poor. Some were very, very poor – impoverished in fact. All these children have been given a chance at life and at hope and it started with one person believing in them. José had a vision of what Venezuela's children could be, beyond the simple reality of what they were.

José Abreu was the conductor of the main orchestra in Caracas when he first shared his vision with members of his own orchestra. Revolted by the increasing numbers of street-children living in slums in the fast expanding Venezuelan capital city, Dr Abreu had a moment of *compulsion*, realizing one day that he had to help these children, and that maybe music could offer them a way out of the slums.

With a few friends and followers around the country, he set about organizing the first rehearsals, setting up the first youth and child orchestras, reaching out into a handful of communities and helping blend rich and poor children together. The government recognized his talent for mobilization, and he was offered the post of Minister for Culture, an opportunity he accepted gladly as it gave him the chance to use his budget and newfound influence to properly fund the program. And fund it he did, putting in place legislation which ensured that the development of music and orchestras became a national priority for Venezuela.

Over the course of the following years, music teachers just like those who had inspired David Serra and his brothers, began to develop the movement. José Abreu was adamant. This was *not* about creating a big national organization. Rather, it was about empowering musicians and teachers locally to create their own orchestras. He and his team shared all the knowledge that was being accumulated, ensured that those who shared his values and vision had access to the tools they needed to grow the movement. As musicians began to emerge to lead the new, child-led renaissance of classical music in Venezuela, Dr Abreu created an orchestra of the orchestras.

The Simon Bolivar Youth Orchestra was designed to be a national and international platform for all budding talents from around the country to hone their skills in a semi-professional environment. The best players from the local and regional ensembles would be given a chance to join the 250-strong Simon Bolivar team, with the hope of being able to play in international concert halls alongside some of the world's greatest soloists.

In 2008, *The Times* of London ran a piece ranking the best orchestras of the world. The top four places were occupied by some of the biggest names in the business – the philharmonics and symphonics of New York, Berlin, and London. But the fifth place was given to an outsider - a group composed of young people, some of whom were barely out of adolescence, and all of whom came from modest and at-risk backgrounds in a small country in Latin America.

Yes, Dr Abreu took El Sistema from a *compulsion* to a reality that has changed over a million lives. He has taken it from humble beginnings in towns like Carona, to the international stage. And he has taken nine year-old schoolboys like David and coached them to become part of one of the top five orchestras in the world.

Organizations tend to be vertical structures, with the leader at the top and a hierarchy separating each layer until you reach the bottom of the pile. The power sits in a centralized fashion with a happy few, and the rest of the organization delivers what the leadership wants. Dr Abreu, who aside from being a musician, conductor and government minister, also found time to develop his passion for economics, could have chosen this model for El Sistema. He could have chosen to build an empire of orchestras and centrally control the learning processes, the schedules, the methodologies, even what is played (much in the way that centralized education systems do all around the world). But he didn't.

His vision was that each orchestra, in each town, in each estate or region, around Venezuela, would be free to establish its own creative space, its own energy and its own unique way of engaging children. Instead of a centralized, controlling structure, Dr Abreu built an empowered, decentralized movement. He laid out the philosophy, he established and shared the vision and the values and he provided the leadership. He mixed his experience with the experience of others and allowed that to be shared. In doing so, he empowered musicians, community workers, conductors, orchestra leaders and more to take up the mantle of El Sistema, adapting it to their local needs and their local environment. His strategy of empowerment allowed El Sistema to grow much faster and much more sustainably than if he had tried to control and govern it.

There is no better illustration of this than one of the stories in the Abreu folklore, which relates how, after a very successful concert in the first years of El Sistema, the maestro was besieged in his dressing room by enthusiastic musicians who wanted to join and support him. He apparently waited patiently until an expectant silence had fallen in the room and then proudly announced that he would accept none of these people to join him. El Sistema was not an organization that needed joining. It was an idea that needed replicating and adapting, and that he would freely share all of the learning, all of the experience, all of the best-practice and knowledge that he had accumulated so others might go forth and start their own orchestra.

It was noted earlier that this is not David's story - that he is our guide. And he is. He has guided us to Dr. José Antonio Abreu and we have discovered a story about the power of one man's vision, about the energy of children, about the deep humanity of both of them, and the method that brought huge change to one country and is now reaching out to so many more around the world.

Over a million children have been supported in their life journey by El Sistema. Many owe their entire lives and futures to it. The country of Venezuela has literally been transformed, and the model is already being developed in the UK, the US, Germany and dozens of other places around the world.

And so, as we return to David, who has long since stopped holding his breath, we find him standing, shouting and whooping in joy as the Simon Bolivar Orchestra complete their third encore with a rendition of the song Mambo, from the musical "42nd Street" that would have had Bernstein himself bopping in the aisles. The players transcending musical excellence to mix it with theatre, pantomime and even slapstick as the fifth best orchestra in the world transforms into a group of kids having a great time (see for yourself by typing Simon Bolivar Mambo into YouTube). David is in a place of memory. In a place of joy. In the past and yet in the present.

"I remember being there, on the stage, with my oboe in my hand. It was such a strong emotion – even today, as a 45 year-old adult, I still get the shivers when I think about it; the learning, the touring, the playing and the friendships. I can honestly tell you that they were the best days of my life. I remember them all, like they were yesterday."

El Sistema was one man's vision - one man's belief that it was possible to fight the greatest of all poverties. This same man trusted that the energy of a generation would make it happen, if only he could empower it.

David again, "It's difficult to leave the memories behind. El Sistema changed my life. It transformed me, gave me bigger hopes and dreams and helped me believe that I could achieve them. I felt that I belonged. The music, the orchestra, they taught me discipline, respect, tolerance. I learned how to listen, not just to the music, but to my parents, to my peers. I learned how to see the world through somebody else's eyes, to accept that they might see the world differently than me. I learned things that I am proud to pass on to my own children. Who knows where I would be today if it were not for El Sistema."

CONCLUSION

What is the journey that change-makers experience? And where do I find myself today in the wake of experiences that others may have had on a similar journey?

Sam Singh shared how he found himself in a situation that created an emotional charge of purpose, unlike anything he had ever experienced in his life. It set him on a course that led to the development of a magnificent school for more than 1200 young girls in rural India. Sam's defining moment came to him in an office tower in New York City. He saw a picture on the front page of the newspaper that shocked him. It was his moment of *compulsion*, a moment when he realized that "I have to" do something.

Ken Shipley is not the kind of guy who stands out in a crowd, but one who is outstanding as a person. Ken's shows us that, beyond the moment of *compulsion*, we need the time to develop the physical, mental and emotional *commitment* to move beyond "I have to" to "I will do," to commit to doing something in the future.

Yet, compulsion and commitment are not enough in themselves. One must have belief in self to act. We need to believe that "I can." We also need the *confidence* that comes from the knowledge that others have travelled this path before us and that there is, indeed, a process in which we can place our trust.

Noerine Kaleeba demonstrates the self-belief that sits within each of us. The confidence that "we can" make a difference. Society is designed to keep us in our place. In order to change it, we must be prepared to bend or challenge the rules, and refute existing ways of seeing things. Noerine's story shows us how to find the energy and how to prepare ourselves to act – even if it seems impossible. She shows us unequivocally the power of self-belief and confidence as foundations for action.

This is the *journey that you take with yourself*.

Karen Hylnsky takes *compulsion*, *commitment* and *confidence* and shows us how they transition into *action*. It is the simplicity of her single life-saving "act" that draws us to her story and incarnates the *transition from you to others*. Nothing happens without *action*. It is the single act that moves intention from the individual to the public. Action moves internal good intentions to external good works.

Through *action* we develop, hone and refine our *vision*, and set the stage for others to join, for the collective to be created and for the seeds of a movement to be sown. The ability to articulate a powerful, inspiring vision and share it at every opportunity, in the way Brother Kelly did, is the key to the transition from the personal to the social – from one to many.

And yet, sharing the vision will come to nought if the *values* are not shared alongside it. After all, it is the values that dress the window and attract in the right type of person. If vision is about moving from one to many, alignment of values is about ensuring that the potential of the many is fully unleashed.

A movement of people who are not aligned in their beliefs and values simply isn't a movement. This is what Veronica, an educator and idealist waging her personal battle for sustained change in a civil society in the Czech Republic, shows us.

To sustain a vision, we share our values and engage those individuals whose values are aligned with ours. We find them, or they find us, we let them know what we're doing or what we want to do and, together, we begin to make it happen.

And finally, when the movement begins to grow · when the energy for change is gathering, the change-maker in us ensures we get out of our own way and *empower* those around us to make the change. These are the steps of the *journey we take with other people*. We enter with *action*, engage with the alignment of shared *vision* and *values*, and *empower* others with the potential to create a movement and change the world for many.

As the final link in the chain, empowerment helps others who share the vision and values claim their power over "the now," and as we see in Mary-Kim's case, power over the future.

This is (me)volution. A journey of transformation. The most important journey you'll ever take.

(me)volution is about you.

It is about your internal journey. It involves you working out what your compulsion really means, and then channelling the energy that is produced into a commitment of a scope that works for you – all the time believing that you can do it.

It is about transitioning your personal commitment into something tangible, something that manifests into action. Then it is about expressing this as a *vision* and then ensuring that you have defined and shared the *values* that drive you so that others can see the *vision* for themselves and align themselves with you and then you can empower them to bring about real change.

And if (me)volution is about you, it is also about the transformation that you have the potential to achieve, should you choose to.

David's story shows how each of the steps in this model can come together to create a passion and a cause so deep, so compelling and so urgent that it grows into something larger than life · bigger than the cause itself. El Sistema gained its own momentum, its own personality and character and became a movement – a movement of absolute change that has transformed the lives of children in both Venezuela and around the world.

And so David's story joins those of Sam, Ken, Noerine, Karen, Brother Kelly, Veronica and Mary-Kim as the guiding beacons on our journey.

We do not believe in absolute truths. Nor do we believe in black and white. These are concepts from a world infinitely less complex than today's global and multi-cultural societies. However, we do believe in the power of models as a basis for thinking and change.

If this book, and the (me)volution model within it -

- has inspired you, or anyone else you know, to have the confidence to not walk away from a compulsion, and to not leave a commitment hanging to "some-day" in a hypothetical future;

- has given you the knowledge that others have trodden the path before you and that you are not alone;

- has meant that you have moved to taking just the first small action;

...then it will have made a difference, because one more person taking more action means one more chance for a vision to develop and a movement to follow it.

If one more person rejects the fear that is inherent within a feeling of compulsion and embraces, however tentatively, the idea that it might just be possible to do something quite remarkable, even as an "ordinary" person, then one more seed has been sown. A seed, that may one day bloom into something powerful and remarkable.

And if, after reading this book, you are able to recognize yourself in it, amongst a group of non-iconic people who are nevertheless world-changers, then you have already taken the first step.

Follow your compulsion, develop your commitment, let your confidence grow, take that very first action and you are on the road to changing your world and that of the people around you for the better.

But don't take our word for it. Take Sam's, Ken's, Karen's, Noerine's, Brother Kelly's, Veronica's, Mary-Kim's and David's, because the process that we have shared with you comes from them.

Now go and change your world, because change begins with us.

POSTSCRIPT

The idea from this book came (as so many do!) from a conversation in a bar in The Netherlands back in 2008. We had just finished a long and intense conference on the future of funding for the non-profit sector, and, fueled by passion, tiredness and perhaps the occasional drop of alcohol, we began wondering if we could define this thing called *philanthropy* in just a few words.

We decided to try, and in doing so, tell stories about philanthropy. Each story would illustrate a different word and be written by a different author.

The chapters began to arrive, stories from around the world, and then it was up to us to fashion them into a book. That's when the fun started, because the authors - Tom, Simone, Kay, Ken, Fraser and Jana - had collectively done much more than write a set of stories. Much, much more.

Instead of eight isolated stories linked by the thread of philanthropy, what we had in our hands was nothing short of a model of how to go from having a good idea to actually changing the world.

Not only was this unexpected, but it meant that we had to write a completely different book. Ignoring what we had been gifted would have been like discovering how to split the atom and choosing to go out for a nice cup of tea instead.

So we wrote this new book.

(me)volution doesn't tell you *how you* will change the world. More, it tells you *the process* others went through when *they* changed the world. We can't all be Gandhi, or Nelson Mandela, or Mother Theresa or Martin Luther King, and we shouldn't try to be. Yet, as the stories in this book prove, we *can* all change the world.

Thank you for reading (me)volution. Visit our website and tell us your story. Work out where you are on the journey and share it with us, and others. Share your experiences as you change the world.

Tony Myers and Jon Duschinsky

Calgary, Toronto, Coboconk, Ontario and finally, Edmonton, Alberta

ABOUT THE AUTHORS

Tony Myers and Jon Duschinsky met at the international fundraising conference in Amsterdam in 2005. They come from very different backgrounds (Tony from Alberta and Jon from France) and indeed from different generations. They have had very different life experiences; but share a powerful vision and passionate set of values.

Tony and Jon both love life and philanthropy. They work hard raising money, building movements and generally trying to make the world a better place. Tony is process oriented with a penchant for detail and analysis. Jon is mad-professor creative – irreverent and edgy in his approach. Both are passionate, enthusiastic, and in-demand presenters. Their skills are complementary and their experiences are too.

But more than anything else, they have loved working together on this book, applying their experiences, knowledge and insight to the inspiring stories of the contributing authors. They were quite sad when this book was finished, and yet excited to take (me)volution out on the road and give the model to the world, while providing themselves with yet another reason to keep working together.

They very much hope that you are able to see their passion through the pages of this book.

ABOUT THE CONTRIBUTORS

Tom Ahern

Tom came late to donor communications, after a distinguished, award-winning career in marketing and journalism. He volunteered for his first non-profit jobs, read more than 150 books on fundraising matters, and eventually emerged as a leading authority on donor newsletters, bequest marketing, direct mail appeals, and case statements.

The Agitator, an influential blog, dubbed Tom a "donor communications guru" in 2011. Each year, Tom delivers dozens of workshops internationally before thousands of fundraisers on the techniques of (and psychology behind) effective fundraising communications. He has authored four well-received how-to books on donor communications, with a fifth underway.

He works with dozens of non-profits each year. In 2011 Tom's clients included international brand names (Catholic Relief Services, Save the Children), major universities (Princeton, University of Calgary), some of America's oldest and biggest charities (Boy Scouts, Volunteers of America), top-tier performance groups (Houston Grand Opera), leading community foundations (New York Community Trust), national advocacy (National Parks Conservation Association, 350,000 members strong), as well as many smaller non-profits.

He has a BA and MA in English from Brown University and a Certificate in Advertising Art from the R.I. School of Design. He and his wife, Simone Joyaux, maintain a second home and writing hideaway in France.

Connect with Tom at http://www.aherncomm.com

Ken Burnett

Ken is an author, lecturer and consultant on fundraising, marketing and communications for non-profit organizations worldwide. In 1982 he founded the influential Burnett Associates agency, which for two decades produced some of the most original, donor-focused and effective communications campaigns to be found anywhere. In the recent past he has worked closely with several communications and marketing agencies in the UK, Australia, North America and India.

Ken is a partner in the transformational development consultancy Clayton Burnett Limited, a director of specialist publishers The White Lion Press Limited and is currently working with fundraisers worldwide to build and develop SOFII, the Showcase of Fundraising Innovation and Inspiration (www.sofii.org).

Ken has served on several non-profit boards including 13 years with the international anti-poverty NGO ActionAid, where he met Noerine Kaleeba. Ken was chairman of ActionAid from 1998 to 2003 and stepped down as independent trustee of ActionAid International, of which he is a founding board member, in 2009. Ken is a former vice chair of The UK's Institute of Fundraising and former trustee of both BookAid International and the International Fund Raising Group (now The Resource Alliance). Ken is a fellow of the Institute of Fundraising in the UK and an honorary fellow of the UK's Institute of Direct Marketing.

A regular writer for websites, magazines and newspapers on both sides of the Atlantic, Ken is author of the worldwide best seller *Relationship Fundraising*, its sequel *Friends for Life,* plus *How to Produce Inspiring Annual Reports, Tiny Essentials of an Effective Volunteer Board* and *The Zen of Fundraising*. All of his books and most articles can be found on the *White Lion Press* website. Ken's first non-fundraising book, *The Field by the River*, was published by Portico books, an imprint of Anova, in hardback in July 2008 with a paperback edition published in 2009.

Ken is a member of the editorial advisory group of *The Raiser's Ask* magazine in South Asia (from Bangalore, India) and of the Editorial Advisory Council for *Advancing Philanthropy* Magazine, the journal of the Association of Fundraising Professionals, in the United States.

In 2007 Ken Burnett was recipient of both *Professional Fundraising* magazine's 'Outstanding Contribution' award and the UK Institute of Fundraising's 'Lifetime Contribution' award.

Connect with Ken at www.kenburnett.com or by email at ken@kenburnett.com.

Jon Duschinsky

Jon is a global leader in marrying social profit with financial profit. From an early age, Jon recognized that people are the most powerful force for driving change in this world. That recognition gave rise to a career dedicated to harnessing that power to activate causes around the world.

For most of the last decade Jon has been involved in pushing the social innovation agenda and envelope across Europe – firstly as the co-founder of the Cascaid agency in the UK at the age of 21, then as head of fundraising of France's largest AIDS organization (Sidaction) before taking on the challenge of being the first ever Director of the French Institute of Fundraising.

In 2008, Jon founded bethechange, a global philanthropic consultancy that provides strategic direction for organizations and companies alike. He is the author of "Philanthropy in a Flat World" (2008), and a celebrated speaker at high-profile international events around the world.

His portfolio contains a diverse array of clients across the globe, and includes the International Red Cross, Amnesty International, the United Nations Development Program, Planet Finance and Children First.

Connect with Jon at jonduschinsky.com.

Kay Sprinkel Grace

Philanthropy is Kay's passion. From her early involvement as a volunteer while pursuing careers in journalism and education, to her evolution as a non-profit fund development manager and then a consultant, her commitment to philanthropy has been her guide.

An accomplished author of six books and highly regarded speaker, she shares her passion globally with people who are seasoned and needing new motivation as well as those new to the field seeking to define the role they can play.

Based in San Francisco, but seeing the world of philanthropy as her platform, Kay has been tireless in working to advance the NGO and non-profit sector. Her seminal work, *Beyond Fundraising*, says it all: our focus needs to be on philanthropy (values-based voluntary giving, asking, joining and serving) and development (of relationships based on shared values and vision). Only then can we fundraise in a way that ensures a values-based process that leads to the growth and impact of long-term donor investment.

Connect with Kay at www.kaygrace.org.

Fraser Green

Fraser is unique in North America with respect to his combined expertise in market research and philanthropy. He is a self-confessed "market research freak" who believes that donors, prospects and members have so much more to tell us if we simply ask them thoughtfully and appropriately.

Fraser is Principal and Chief Strategist at Good Works, one of Canada's leading fundraising consulting agencies. At Good Works, Fraser's focus is on deep human communication, donor research and legacy giving. Prior to coming to consulting in 1996, Fraser was CEO of the New Democratic Party of Canada, Special Assistant to Ontario Premier Bob Rae and Director of Organization for the Ontario NDP.

Fraser is a gifted writer and a sought-after public speaker. He presents regularly at fundraising conferences in Canada, the USA and Europe. His articles and contrarian rants (as he calls them) are frequently published in professional journals. Fraser is the co-author of *Iceberg Philanthropy* (2007), and author of the recently published *3D Philanthropy*.

Fraser has a BA in Economics from St. Mary's University in Halifax and did his graduate studies in Social Policy and Administration at Carleton University in Ottawa.

In his spare time, Fraser is passionate about his guitars and banjo, kayaking, yoga, cross-country skiing, cycling, reading and talking too much. The new loves of his life are his two Labrador Retrievers – a chocolate female named "Oonagh" (rhymes with tuna) and a black male named "Handsome Jack."

Fraser and his wife Jennifer live with their two boys in a log house outside Ottawa. His daughter Rory has just finished her BA in political science at UBC and has already started to change the world as a fundraiser with the Canadian Cancer Society.

Connect with Fraser at fraser@goodworksco.ca

Simone P. Joyaux, ACFRE

Simone is an expert in fund development, strategic planning, and governance/board development. She provides these services to all types and sizes of non-profits. Joyaux serves as faculty for the Masters Program in Philanthropy and Development at Saint Mary's University of Minnesota, and speaks at conferences worldwide.

As a volunteer, Joyaux regularly serves on boards. She founded the Women's Fund of Rhode Island, a social justice organization, and chaired the CFRE International Board when it became an independent corporation.

Her books, *Keep Your Donors: The Guide to Better Communications and Stronger Relationships* and *Strategic Fund Development: Building Profitable Relationships That Last* (co-authored with Tom Ahern) receives rave reviews. The 3rd edition of Strategic Fund Development – considered a standard in the sector – was released in March 2011. Simone is also a web columnist for The Non-profit Quarterly.

Professionals and volunteers describe Joyaux as "one of the most thoughtful, inspirational, and provocative leaders" in the philanthropic sector. She and her life partner Tom Ahern, give away at least 10% of their income annually, and have bequeathed their entire estate to charity.

Connect with Simone at www.simonejoyaux.com.

Jana Ledvinová, Ing.

As Executive Director (until 2003) Jana was responsible for internal and external management and the long-term development strategy for the organization known as Tereza. Tereza put together a strong mission and strategy to support environmental awareness and help to grow the new and fragile civil society of the Czech Republic democracy after 1989. During the last 30 years Tereza has became a professional non-profit organization, providing services for more than 20% of all schools and local community groups in the Czech Republic.

As an international trainer and consultant, Jana has been providing training and consultations in fundraising, personal management, strategic planning, marketing, advocacy and partnership building in more than 20 countries, mostly in the CEE region. Most recently she has utilized her long-term experiences from working with countries and organizations in transition for the Resource Alliance, UK.

Connect with Jana at janaledvinova@volny.cz

Tony Myers, Ph.D., M.A., LL.B., CFRE

Tony is a passionate student of philanthropy. He believes deeply in its power to change the world. He is dedicated to the discipline of development; teaching others about it while still loving the front lines of fundraising.

Tony works every day to help organizations (large or small, local and international) to focus their energies, develop winning strategies, and raise more money. His skill is in major gift fundraising, capital campaigns, board development and strategic planning.

With twenty years of experience and after numerous campaigns, Tony knows what it takes to win, and why we sometimes fail.

He has spoken and made presentations on four continents. His spirited presentations make you think, and sometimes touch the soul, as well as the heart.

Tony walks the talk. He is the founder and Principal Counsel for Myers & Associates. His involvement in the non-profit sector includes experience on several boards: CFRE International (the accreditation body for the fundraising profession) the Association of Fundraising Professionals, Calgary Chapter, the Association of Fundraising Professionals, Edmonton chapter, CentrePoint for Non-profit Management, the Kelsey Institute Foundation, the ASTech Foundation, Public Legal Information Services, Sustainable Calgary, and other non-profit organizations in across Canada.

His work has been recognized through national and international awards. He has written articles for *Canadian Fundraising & Philanthropy*, is a contributing author to the best-selling book *"Excellence in Fundraising in Canada"* and also completed a chapter for *"Fundraising Feasibility Studies."*

Contact Tony at Tony@MyersCan.com

Printed by Publishers Graphics Canada Inc